How *Hot* is Your Product?

FIND OUT IF YOUR PRODUCT IDEA
WILL *MAKE* OR *COST* YOU MONEY!

SAVE THOUSANDS OF DOLLARS BY
ASKING THE RIGHT QUESTIONS FIRST!

DR. TAMARA MONOSOFF AND BRAD KOFOED

HOW HOT IS YOUR PRODUCT?

Find out if your product idea will make or cost you money!

By Tamara Monosoff and Brad Kofoed

© 2013-2014 Start Up Smarts Academy Press

Start Up Smarts Academy Press
P.O. Box 908
Orinda, CA 94563

DEDICATION

We are dedicating this book to our precious daughters, Sophia and Kiara.
You are our greatest creations!

Acknowledgments

We want to extend our appreciation and gratitude to the hundreds of inventors and entrepreneurs we have worked with over the years. You have been our friends and teachers. We have written this guidebook for you and those following in your creative footsteps.

When we started out ten years ago, we didn't have the answers to the critical questions provided in this book. We went through the product development process, designing, patenting, manufacturing, and shipping. In some cases, we ended up with hundreds of units of various products in our garage—and later warehouses—that we couldn't sell because we didn't understand the market.

We learned that some products hit it big quickly while others do well over time. And, some never achieve an entrepreneur's dreams or goals. While there is no crystal ball we can give you, there are many ways to uncover clues and evidence as to the business opportunity your product presents.

We want to share lessons we learned to help entrepreneurs avoid our mistakes. A few years ago, after many requests, we began offering a product evaluation consulting program. Over and over again we came away with phenomenal insights that we shared with the inventors who participated in the program. However, we found that the program was cost prohibitive for many aspiring inventors, and for us, it was too difficult to deliver because of the extensive number of hours it took to carefully evaluate each product. Therefore, we expanded and refined our program and created this 10 Step

Guidebook to make it accessible to any inventor who is serious about pursuing his or her product ideas.

In this guidebook we provide you with the best possible questions that will help you gain clarity and knowledge about you and your product's potential. Going through this process will give you a distinct advantage and help you make better decisions that will have a direct impact on your life.

We wish to thank Erika Ruggiero for her magnificent design work for the cover and interior layout for this book, and my friends, Tamarah Haet and Annette Giacomazzi, for their insights and editing that helped improve this book.

Finally, this section would be incomplete if we didn't acknowledge each other. We have been together for 26 years. During that time, we have supported each other's many projects and most importantly created a family together that we cherish.

Creating this guidebook has been especially gratifying because we've been in the trenches together for years, yet this is our first co-authored book. We share a conviction to truly serve people. Our purpose is to help you avoid costly mistakes, increase the speed of your success, and facilitate the achievement of your own dreams.

ALSO BY DR. TAMARA MONOSOFF:

The Mom Inventors Handbook: How to Turn Your Great Idea into the Next Big Thing (McGraw-Hill, 2005).

Secrets of Millionaire Moms: Learn How They Turned Great Ideas into Booming Businesses – and How You Can Too! (McGraw-Hill, 2007).

The One Page Business Plan for Women in Business (co-authored with Jim Horan, President of the One Page Business Plan Company, 2010).

Your Million Dollar Dream: Regain Control & Be Your Own Boss (McGraw-Hill, 2010).

CONNECT ONLINE:

Starting and Building a Business?
Meet Tamara online and receive training at:
www.TamaraMonosoff.com and **www.MomInvented.com**

CONNECT WITH TAMARA:

Twitter: @TamaraMonosoff
Twitter: @MomInventors
Facebook: http://www.facebook.com/monosoff
Facebook: www.facebook.com/mominvented
Linked In: www.linkedin.com/pub/tamara-monosoff/4/855/2a6

CONNECT WITH BRAD:
Twitter: @BradKofoed
Linked In: http://www.linkedin.com/pub/brad-kofoed/4/898/31

If you have questions, you are welcome to email us at:
info@TamaraMonosoff.com.

WHAT YOU WILL DISCOVER IN THIS GUIDEBOOK:

Welcome! You have taken an important step. Objectively assessing whether your product is worth pursuing is critical to your success and happiness. Why? Because taking a product to market is both risky and hard work. Self-confidence, commitment, stamina, and courage in the face of doubt are essential for an entrepreneur to succeed. And, taking your own product from the kernel of an idea to store shelves may be one of the most rewarding things you do professionally. However, this is a unique time in your life when some measured self-doubt is healthy. Therefore, the best way to manage risk is to become knowledgeable by getting the answers you need to make smart and thoughtful decisions about your next steps. YOU are the best person to do this.

A business plan will improve the likelihood of success of any project or business, especially one as challenging as a product business. However, before you write a plan or create the product itself, very careful evaluation is necessary. It is important to take the steps to evaluate the viability of your product **BEFORE** you dive in and spend a lot of money. This will set you apart from most product entrepreneurs.

We often hear, "This product is my baby!" Although you need passion and dedication to create a successful business, "defending your baby" makes you susceptible to not hearing the "truth" about your product. You may love your product idea, but we have some tough love for you: **Your product does _not_ care about you and never will … unlike a "baby."**

Tamara learned the hard way about the cost of bringing her product to market. "It cost over $20,000 to bring my first product, the TP Saver™ (prevents kids from pulling the toilet paper) to market. The costs included samples, prototypes, engineering drawings, graphics, packaging design, logo creation and design, manufacturing, trade shows, safety testing, liability insurance, and marketing materials. If you had told me this in the beginning, I most likely would not have begun. I didn't have $20,000 sitting in the bank. In fact, when I started out, I didn't have any money put aside. Each time there was a new cost I felt tremendous stress and had to figure out how I was going to pay for it. And, I had no idea if the product was going to be a success or not."

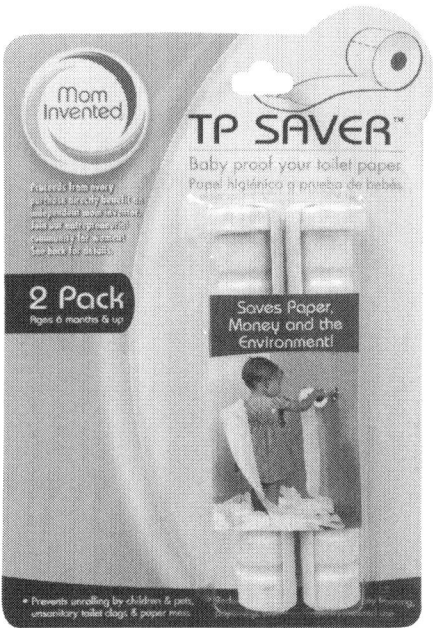

Taking that product to market taught us a lot. Today, presented with an objective assessment of the opportunity (market + profit) – (financial investment + personal resources), we would have passed on that product idea. "Why?" you might ask.

The TP Saver served a very niche market. At about $1 gross profit per unit, we would have had to sell a million units to clear $1 million gross profit (not "net" profit). We sold fewer than 100,000 units. In hindsight, had we put ourselves through these 10 steps, we would have understood the limited marketability and focused our money and resources on business ideas with greater potential (e.g., either a larger potential market or a higher per-unit gross margin—ideally both!).

Although the TP Saver did not meet our financial goals at the time, we learned a great deal from the process, which enabled us to launch other products and build a company. In other words, we derived other benefits from the experience.

Here's Another Way to Look at Inventing

Pretend you are on a product development team for a large company, like Kimberly Clark or Proctor & Gamble, and you need to present an evaluation for a new product to the executive team (a.k.a., your boss). You know your job will be on the line if you don't carefully review the product idea for its potential success and present all the information a critical executive team facing a major investment would expect. Take this view: **"This product must *prove itself* to me before I am willing to invest my time and money in its development."**

With that in mind, take a deep breath because you are an entrepreneur, which means that *you* are both the researcher *and* the boss! You will need to be careful and diligent in the way you learn about your product's potential. As with all entrepreneurs, your optimism and enthusiasm are important when it comes to overcoming the challenges you will face launching your business. But at this stage, your energy needs to be channeled and focused on this process so that you can feel confident and clear about whether it makes sense to invest your time and money in this endeavor.

In this process, we will ask you to wear different hats. The first is a detective's hat. Using the techniques that we outline, you will need to become a researcher who finds and follows information. As you discover pieces of data, note them and set them aside. The second hat is that of a puzzle master. You will assemble the pieces of information so that the story they tell is as clear as possible. This may sound difficult. It is. One of the challenges of launching a truly new product is that it hasn't been done before, which is why they call it "inventing." This is why most people don't do it and why many products fail. Oftentimes, the products shouldn't have been taken to market to begin with. So, in many circumstances, such as our TP Saver example, the failure was not in the product development and launch but in the prior analysis—or lack thereof.

However, you *can* do this. Don't worry if you can't answer every question. The goal here is to gather as much information as possible. And don't be surprised if you actually find the process to be fascinating!

As you begin the steps, keep in mind that if this current idea fails to prove itself to you, you've actually succeeded! Move on to the next great opportunity in which you can invest your time and energy. On the other hand, if you find that your idea represents a business opportunity worthy of your commitment and investment, then go forward and create your business plan knowing that you have done all that you can to make good decisions.

Onward!

INSTRUCTIONS:

When we do product evaluations, we expect to spend between 15 and 30 hours on each one. It took us longer in the beginning, but we did not have this guidebook when we started the process either. Block out time for each section and keep the following in mind: While you may be tempted to dive into the product development process, taking a week or two beforehand to go through the 10 Steps provided here will (a) improve your pace and level of success if you choose to proceed, and (b) save you thousands of dollars and months of your life if you learn that this product will not be financially viable.

Each of the following steps has a heading that addresses one of the key points we use for evaluating the viability of a new product. The temptation will be to fill it out based on "instinct," personal views, and feedback from family and friends. Except where specifically noted in the "Background" section, we want you to be specific, based on real data that you gather. For any claim, statement, or conclusion that you make about the product, you must be able to answer the second follow-up question: **"How do you know?"** If, as that product developer for a large company, you would not feel comfortable answering that second question with confidence, reassess the initial conclusion, claim, or statement and, if necessary, dig deeper.

BACKGROUND:
PRODUCT SUMMARY INFORMATION

WHERE ARE YOU IN THE PROCESS RIGHT NOW?

> **The purpose of this section is to get you started with what you have today and to document your thoughts right now, before you go through the 10 steps in this guidebook. Even if you don't know the answers, just make your best guess.**

PRODUCT NAME: (A WORKING NAME OR DESCRIPTIVE TITLE IS OK AT THIS STAGE.)

Opus and Zooey   Childrens Pajamas w/ a removable feet & reverse zipper

PRODUCT DESCRIPTION:

In one to three sentences, succinctly describe the product here.

A new take on footy pajamas. The zipper will start at the top and close down provide easy access for diaper changes while keeping baby warm and covered. Removable feet will be attached to pajamas for warmth, but can be flipped back if they need to be removed. They are attached to pajamas.

Write the 3-5 key features and benefits of the product:

Features (What is it made of? Is it durable? Chemical free?
Locally made/grown? What color? Stylish? Lightweight?
Easily Cleaned? Inexpensive? Interchangeable?)

✓ Reverse zipper for coverage & diaper access

✓ Flip feet

✓ Made in USA

✓ 100% organic cotton

✓

Benefits (What problem does it solve? Does it save money?
Save time? Create joy? Reduce pain? Improve
health/happiness?)

✓ Keeps upper half of baby covered & warm while
   changing diaper

✓ Babies can't pull of feet (socks), but allows removal
✓ for feet exposure
   traction

✓ feeds US economy

✓

"WHO" specifically will buy it? Avoid broad terms and descriptions like, "Everyone in America" or "All Women" or "All Kids" … These are overly broad terms and are unrealistic.

New parents (young, hip) in Urban, hip areas ... the coasts Parents who want the organic, super soft product touching their baby in the first year of their life. Parents who are "in the know" about baby products and only want the best.

How much will he/she pay for it?

$35 - 50

"WHY" will this customer buy? How do you know?

All of their household products are organic, locally made, boutique supplied, no chemicals Meyers, Aiden & Anais

We asked you to answer these questions to give you a starting point from which you can measure your progress. By the end of this guidebook, you will be able to see what you've learned and how your thinking may have shifted or evolved.

The next section is the first of the 10 Steps. At the end of each of the steps, you will be asked to rank your product based on what you've learned in each specific section. And at the very end of the book, you will be given the opportunity to gather all of your rankings into one organized summary sheet. This will help you evaluate your product overall so that you can thoughtfully decide what to do next.

STEP 1: SELF-ASSESSMENT: WHAT ARE YOUR PERSONAL GOALS?

> The purpose of this section is to help you gain clarity about what you want and your personal strengths and challenges. These answers are still free form. If you don't know, just make your best guess.

It is important to think about what you want to build from the beginning. At this stage, you may not know exactly what you want to do with the product. That is fine. This may be challenging because there are so many unanswered questions. Take a shot anyway. By the time you get through the entire process, you will be able to clarify your initial thoughts.

Is this a hobby or a serious business endeavor?

At the moment it feels like a hobby (another thing I'm interested in) but I'd like it to become a serious business endeavor.

Is it your goal to build a product manufacturing and distribution business?

NO

Is your goal to license the product to another company?
(Licensing means you sell your idea to another manufacturer
who will make the product, and you will earn a small
percentage—usually 2-5%—or "royalty" on the net sales
instead of making the product and becoming a manufacturer
yourself. Note: If licensing is the preferred path, the ability to
attain intellectual property—a patent—is important.) [See
Step 4 for Patent Information.]

_NO_

Or do you have a different goal?

Be a company owner

**Do you have specific financial goals or requirements that
will determine whether you will pursue this project?**

_I want to be able to bring in
a profit and grow from this_

How much money have you set aside to develop the product and invest in your business?

$5K

_____

_____

_____

_____

How much outside funding will you need to build your business?

$5k

_____

_____

_____

_____

It's also important to consider other goals beyond financial rewards: *Flexibility, Creativity, I come up with ideas and others make & ship. liesure, freedom*

Risk.

How much risk can you tolerate? Some people can tolerate tremendous risk while others have no stomach for it. When you start a business, you need to understand where you fall in this "risk tolerance" continuum. For example, know how much you are willing to spend and at what point you are willing to walk away.

First, complete the **Risk Continuum Exercise** (next page) and then describe (below) your own risk comfort level here.

I am very comfortable with taking risks. I am resourceful, tenacious, scrappy and I get the job done. I am willing to work long hours with low pay for a challenging & creative payoff. The financial investment makes me nervous. I do not have money to lose ... but I do have everything to gain. I am a fast learner & tend to take risks in my life

We met a woman recently who has spent $80,000 on her prototype, patenting, and marketing for her product business. She is still not selling her product and has not put a realistic plan in place. To us, this is way too risky.

REALITY & RISK CONTINUUM

What is your level of risk tolerance?
Where do you fall on a continuum?

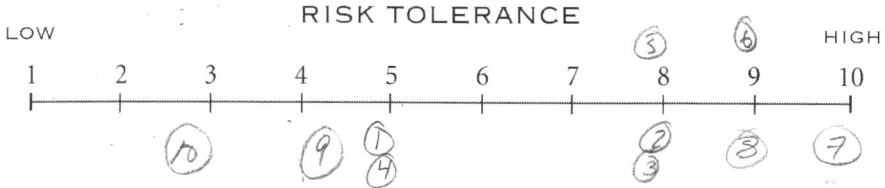

RISK TOLERANCE

LOW   HIGH

1	2	3	4	5	6	7	8	9	10

Instructions:

This exercise is intended to bring clarity by providing you with a visual display of your personal risk profile as it relates to this project. The upside of taking risk can be extraordinary success in many forms: financial, freedom, relationships, leisure, etc.

That said, by nature, "risk" means that there can be negative consequences to a project. It is not our intention to unnecessarily focus on this aspect, or to convince you that you should not accept the risk and proceed, but rather, to help you be fully mindful in the process of accepting risk. Too often, we have witnessed, and experienced ourselves, the tendency to put on blinders to potential risks when there is excitement about a new project. (In our own work, we now see a candid risk assessment as a useful mechanism to help choose between multiple exciting options to pursue.)

Take a different colored pen or marker and place a mark on the continuum based on your answer to each question or statement below. A strong "no" to the statements would place you at or near the "1". Absolute or strong "yes" puts you toward the "10". This is not scientific and you can even add questions that are specifically relevant to you. You decide where each mark goes. Then consider what you see.

Questions:

1) I can afford to lose the money I will be investing in this business.

2) I am comfortable working long hours, for months, with very low pay.

3) I am comfortable with major changes on a regular basis.

4) I have a family and/or solid support system I can rely upon to help tackle the big challenges.

5) I thrive on pressure.

6) I just learned I will appear on national television in three days. I am 1) paralyzed – 10) thrilled.

7) If my business took off and the pace and priorities of my life changed within a few months, I would be 1) displeased – 10) very satisfied.

8) I will be fine if key relationships in my life are impacted by this process.

9) I am comfortable asking people to invest or lend me money.

10) I am comfortable dealing with legal matters and possible disputes.

Effort.

How much time and effort are you willing and able to spend on this product business? Please be realistic.

I can work all day on weekends, early morning & morning on Tuesdays & late night the rest of the week.

Are you working full-time? Are you a single parent? Are you caring for your aging parents? Look at your schedule and analyze how much time you can realistically block out to work on your business each day and week. (See the chart on the next page.) Actually list which hours and days you would use and then test this plan to gauge if those times are working for the next two weeks.

Is it sustainable for two years? If it's not working, adjust your schedule. Do everything you can to create consistency with your schedule. Think of this like a job.

TIME	SUNDAY	MONDAY	TUESDAY	WEDNESDAY	THURSDAY	FRIDAY	SATURDAY
EARLY MORNING			✓				
LATE MORNING	✓		✓				✓
EARLY AFTERNOON	✓						✓
LATE AFTERNOON/ EVENING	✓	✓		✓	✓		✓
LATE EVENING							

Work style.

What is your work style? Some entrepreneurs feel lonely working on their projects and want to be surrounded by others. Others can work alone all day in a home office and be fine. Know your own preferences so that you can factor this into your planning.

I prefer to collaborate and work with others. I can work on my own when I'm surrounded by others - possibly a coffee shop or communal office space.

Lifestyle.

Think about the lifestyle you want to create. Don't overlook the stress of success. Sometimes success means less time with your family because you are working all the time, making complex decisions with investors and customers. What aspects of your lifestyle are important to you? What do you want to keep? What do you envision will change?

1. Currently have no social ties ... work away!

GAIN INSIGHTS ABOUT YOUR OWN PERSONAL BUSINESS POSTURE

> **The purpose of this section is for you to ask yourself about your own personal business strengths and where you may need extra support.**

Write the value in each box so that they can be added up. In other words, if you have a lot of experience in building a business, write a "5" in the box across from that section under the "5" for Advantage. If you have no business experience, write a "1" beneath the "1" heading in that section. Combine the subtotals to get your Total number.

		Challenge		Neutral	Advantage	
	VALUE	**1**	**2**	**3**	**4**	**5**
1	**Experience Building a Business**	1				
2	**Access to Capital**			3		
3	**Customer Knowledge**			3		
4	**Product Industry Knowledge**		2			
5	**Support, e.g. Family**			3		
6	**Available Work Time**			3		
7	**Financial Stability and Access to Resources**	1				
8	**Passion/Drive**				4	
	Subtotal					

TOTAL: 20

What is your total? A score of 17-24 is considered neutral. A score that's less than 24 does not mean you shouldn't move forward. Many successful entrepreneurs and innovators created their businesses out of thin air. This is merely an effort to take stock of where you are today with regards to your assets and strengths and to make you aware of where you may need some extra support.

RANK WHERE YOU FALL IN POINTS:
(CIRCLE 1, 2, OR 3)

UNDER 16	17-24	25-40
1	2	3

In the next step we shift from "you" to the potential market for your product.

STEP 2: MARKET:
WHAT IS THE REALISTIC, TARGETABLE MARKET FOR YOUR PRODUCT?

> **The purpose of this section is to determine, with as much accuracy as possible, the estimated size (qualified consumers) of your potential market.**

One way to determine your potential market is to develop numbers that can help you formulate your likely target customer base. Each market is different. Your data points will be unique as well. We've designed a way to chart this information so that you can create a visual picture. The intention of this tool is to help you move from broad information to specific data. You will want to get as specific as possible about the nature of the customer, placing that information in the center for each market. There is a completed example for one market (juvenile market) at the end of this section for your review. (See page 42.)

We want to acknowledge that there will clearly be overlap between this step and the next. We are piecing together a jigsaw puzzle and when you assemble a puzzle, sometimes you look at it from different angles and build different sections until they all come together. In this step, the idea is to quantify the actual size of the potential market, whereas the next section approaches this from the perspective of the benefit to the customer, in as measurable a means as possible.

1. Who is the target customer? Describe the person who will be pulling out their wallet to pay for your product.

2. How many of these kinds of customers exist? (Note: While theoretically the market can be global, we consider the US market to be the best measure of this metric for American inventors. (Below you can see how you can begin gathering this information at www.Census.gov.)

3. Working from the outside of the target chart and looking in (reference pages 42 and 51), think through and note the descriptive characteristics of this customer using the following list to help you think of the key traits.

    The number of rings in your target chart can be increased as you identify additional filters to place on your target market. Then, like cutting a pizza, segment the circle based on different markets in which you intend to sell your product.
    a. Gender
    b. Age / Generation
    c. Race
    d. Geographic location and needs (e.g., more people buy mittens in Michigan than in Florida)
    e. Urban / Suburban dweller. Think about the differences. For example, just consider the driving, gardening, shopping—you name it— habits and needs of these types of consumers.
    f. Economic class
    g. Professional / Blue Collar / Student
    h. Parent / Non-parent
    i. Educational level
    j. Other characteristics applicable to your product/category
        i. Active/ Athletic
        ii. Use of technology
        iii. Hobbies
        iv. Traveler
        v. Pet owners
        vi. Other

The US Census Office website (http://www.census.gov) has a wealth of information that will help you identify your market. It takes some time (and patience) to sift through the data to find useful numbers, so be prepared to spend some time to find precisely what you are seeking. Once you get used to the way the website is organized, the data is quite interesting. This data is especially useful if your product is specifically relevant to particular populations based on demographic specifics such as age, gender, geography, or ethnicity. For example, we know that there are approximately 117 million total US households, of which 71 million are "family" households. Approximately 38 million households have children under 18 years. Also interesting is that over 30 percent of American households are in just four states: California, Texas, Florida, and New York.

4. How much money is spent annually in the product category? How much money is spent on similar or comparable items?

5. Using search engines, type, "____ market statistics," "sales of ____," and experiment with other search terms. Another often overlooked approach is to simply type your question into a search engine such as Google. For example, "How many ____ are there in America?" Be sure and cross reference (check facts against multiple sources) to make sure the information you gather is reliable.

6. Look up the industry association that represents the market space your item falls into and read their market statistics. Type your "category + association" into Google to find them. Search trade publication websites that serve this market and read their statistics. For example, if you are looking for the National Pet Association but don't

know the exact name, type that phrase into a search engine. When we put "National Pet Association" into Google, it took us immediately to American Pet Products Association: http://www.americanpetproducts.org/. You can do this with any industry, and you will often find a plethora of invaluable data to help you understand the market you are trying to reach.

This is just a portion of the AMAZING data available at the *American Pet Products Association* website:

Industry Statistics & Trends

PET OWNERSHIP

- According to the 2011-2012 APPA National Pet Owners Survey, 62% of U.S. households own a pet, which equates to 72.9 millions homes

- In 1988, the first year the survey was conducted, 56% of U.S. households owned a pet as compared to 62% in 2008

Breakdown of pet ownership in the U.S. according to the 2011-2012 APPA National Pet Owners Survey

Number of U.S. Households that Own a Pet (millions)

Bird	5.7
Cat	38.9
Dog	46.3
Equine	2.4
Freshwater Fish	11.9
Saltwater Fish	0.7
Reptile	4.6
Small Animal	5.0

Total Number of Pets Owned in the U.S. (millions)

Bird	16.2
Cat	86.4
Dog	78.2
Equine	7.9
Freshwater Fish	151.1
Saltwater Fish	8.61
Reptile	13.0
Small Animal	16.0

* Ownership statistics are gathered from APPA's 2011-2012 National Pet Owners Survey

Now, try to answer the question, "How many of these customers in the key market experience the problem or will have their need solved by this product?"

_____

_____

_____

_____

7. As an independent, small entrepreneur, it is important to leverage other people's efforts as much as possible. Just like we will show you in Step 4 (how to take advantage of the legal work completed by other peoples' attorneys), we are going to show you how to get market insights from experienced teams at the biggest companies in your industry.

There are specific websites that gather detailed information about companies and their key employees (http://www.zoominfo.com and http://www.hoovers.com). Not only can you learn a lot about the specific company you are researching, but these sites also list companies considered to be their top competitors. Follow this path until you find relevant corporate information.

Follow these steps:

✓ Find companies (or at least one company) in the market that manufactures items similar to yours. Make a list of these companies and write down the products that you've identified that seem comparable to yours. (Note: If the company is public, visit their homepage and research their sales. (You can gather sales information only from publicly traded companies. Private companies usually do not reveal this information.)

✓ Visit each company's website on the "Related Companies" List (shown above).

✓ Once there, read their Press Page for news releases about products and sales. Read as many as you can to see what you can find. Finding one new kernel of information is worth the time and effort.

✓ Find some public companies among them. Public companies always have "Investor Information" links as well. These will usually provide access to the company's annual report and links to public filings.

For example, if we wanted to invent or create a new kind of gardening shears, we would physically go to different stores in our local area to see what products are currently on store shelves.

Here's a photo of a pair of garden shears from our local True Value store. Now, become a detective.

This may be a good retailer for you to pitch your product to later. Look at the price point. If the product is selling for $24.99, by how much will this manufacturer have to reduce their costs in order to still make money? (See Step 10.) Notice how the product is packaged. This will help you get an idea as to how you might like to package your product.

Later, you can send this photo to a factory, and they will be able to give you a realistic estimate as to the cost of packaging your product. Most factories, especially those overseas, will handle the packaging of your product as well as the production of the product. They will say something like the product will cost $2 per unit to produce and the packaging will be an additional $.34 per unit.

Now, become a detective and flip the product over to see if it's patented and who the manufacturer is. When you go home, get busy sleuthing out information about the manufacturer. Find out what other stores they sell their product to and add any other essential pieces of information you can find to your puzzle to help deepen your understanding.

Make sure you get the maximum benefit from your research. While the specific purpose here is to gain knowledge of your target market, there are other benefits to be had. For example, at some point you may pursue a licensing strategy (selling your product to another manufacturer). While looking up the companies note the size of their product lines and read their press releases and management biographies to see if they may be a good licensing partner prospect. Also, look to see if they could potentially be your competitor so that you can bring a product to market that is different and fills a need that their products are not fulfilling.

Here's an example of how to learn more about this company. Go to www.ZoomInfo.com and type in **Corona Clipper Inc.,** which you found on the product package in the True Value store (photo right).

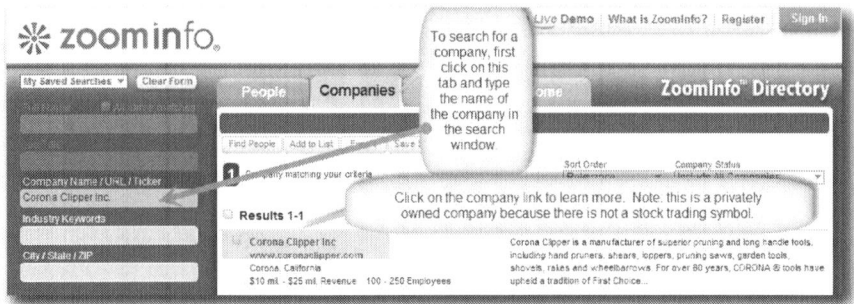

Flip the package over and find the manufacturer's contact information. Visit their website (www.coronatoolsusa.com) to see what you can learn.

CORONA.

Corona Clipper Inc.
22440 Temescal Canyon Rd. • Corona, CA 92883
(951) 737-6515 • (800) 847-7863 • FAX: (951) 737-8657
coronatoolsusa.com
© 2011 Corona Clipper Inc.

Assembled in Mexico from component parts from USA, Taiwan and Vietnam
Ensamblado en México de partes hechas en EE.UU., Taiwan y Vietnam

※ zoominfo.

Live Demo | What is ZoomInfo? | Register | Sign In

My Saved Searches ▼ | Clear Form

People | Companies | ome | **ZoomInfo® Directory**

To search for a company, first click on this tab and type the name of the company in the search window.

Find People | Add to List | Save

Company matching your criteria

Company Name / URL / Ticker
Corona Clipper Inc

Industry Keywords

City / State / ZIP

Sort Order | Company Status

☐ Results 1-1

Click on the company link to learn more. Note, this is a privately owned company because there is not a stock trading symbol.

Corona Clipper Inc
www.coronaclipper.com
Corona, California
$10 mil - $25 mil Revenue 100 - 250 Employees

Corona Clipper is a manufacturer of superior pruning and long handle tools, including hand pruners, shears, loppers, pruning saws, garden tools, shovels, rakes and wheelbarrows. For over 80 years, CORONA ® tools have upheld a tradition of First Choice...

The Corona Clipper example shows the process of working from an actual product. Another approach for gaining market-specific information is to look directly at well-known, large public companies in the same industry.

For example, we know that Central Garden & Pet Company is a public company in this same industry, so we want to also look them up. The steps to investigate a public company are different, but it is usually a great opportunity to get much more detailed market research.

This is a great way to get the company's contact information that is not always easy to find on their website.

Here we can learn the key industry words associated with this company. This can be used to do another search using these words to dig deeper.

This is an incredible way to identify other similar companies in the industry.

Now you can dig deeper to learn more about your industry by going to the company's annual report. If the company is public they have to make this information available. Look at the Table of Contents to find the Market information.

Keep in mind that we are still adding pieces to our puzzle. First, we looked Central Garden & Pet Company up on www.ZoomInfo.com to see what we could learn. Then we visited their website directly. On their website, we first perused their press page then clicked on "investors," where we found their annual report. Usually these documents have "market" sections and describe their competition, distribution, and other highly relevant topics. Note how much you can learn about an industry and a company in a couple of paragraphs.

When you find a listing of a company in your category that lists their NAICS code, write down the code. (NAICS stands for North American Industry Classification System, and it is the standard created by the United States Census Bureau to help collect information on the American economy and how the various industrial sectors affect the economy. Source: eHow.com.) This number will be helpful in other future research steps. You will see above that Central Garden & Pet Company's NAICS Code is 335121,311111.

To see how we benefited by digging deeper into this company, on the next page is a sample excerpt from Central Garden & Pet's annual report that contains data that could be relevant to an inventor developing a product in this industry.

If we want more data on the company and want to read other public filings, we typically go to www.Yahoo.com/finance to access data about companies there.

Garden Products Business

Overview

We are a leading company in the consumer lawn and garden market in the United States and offer both premium and value-oriented branded products. We market and produce a broad array of premium brands, including Pennington, The Rebels, AMDRO, Grant's, Lilly Miller, Ironite, Sevin, Over'n Out, Norcal Pottery, New England Pottery, GKI/Bethlehem Lighting and Matthews Four Seasons. We also produce value brands at lower prices, including some Wal*Mart private label brands. In addition, Garden Products operates a sales and logistics network that strategically supports its brands. In fiscal 2011, Garden Products accounted for $777.3 million of our consolidated net sales and $50.0 million of our consolidated income from operations before corporate expenses and eliminations.

Industry Background

We believe that gardening is one of the most popular leisure activities in the United States, although in recent years our garden segment has been adversely impacted by the global recessionary economic environment. Packaged Facts asserts that the economy has brought more homeowners into their yards. The key demographic bolstering our lawn and garden market is the growth rate in the number of adults over age 55, who are more likely to be "empty nesters" and have more disposable income and leisure time available for garden activities. As the baby boom generation ages, this segment is expected to grow faster than the total population. According to U.S. census data, 42% of the population will be 45 years or older in 2015. We believe that this demographic should increase the number of lawn and garden product users. With more people gardening in their yards and the potential trends of food gardening and organic gardening, we perceive this market as staying intact and showing slow positive growth. We estimate the retail sales of the lawn and garden supplies industry in the categories in which we participate to be approximately $6 billion. We believe that the industry will continue to grow, albeit potentially at a slower rate in the near term due to recessionary pressures in the broader U.S. economy.

Lawn and garden products are sold to consumers through a number of distribution channels, including home centers, mass merchants, independent nurseries and hardware stores. Home and garden centers and mass merchants often carry one or two premium product lines or brands and one value brand. Due to the rapid expansion and consolidation of mass merchants and home and garden centers in the last 15 years, the concentration of purchasing power for the lawn and garden category has increased dramatically. We expect the growth of home and garden centers, such as Home Depot and Lowe's, and mass merchants, such as Wal*Mart, to continue to concentrate industry distribution.

LOOK WHAT WE JUST FOUND!

By going to Yahoo Finance, we found a link to another quarterly report for the same company. There we uncovered great data about the size of both the pet and garden markets.

At this point you should be getting a picture of the size of the potential market for your product.

NOTE: Get legal advice before posting your product publicly (such as on a website, chat room, blog, etc.) absent a verbal or written confidential agreement or provisional application unless you have no intention of pursuing patent rights. Once you disclose publicly (non-confidential disclosure of your invention), there is a risk of damaging your patentability rights since the clock starts ticking and you have only one year to file with the United States Patent & Trademark Office. We know many companies that seldom bother with high-cost patents because they have no intention of licensing their products. Depending on your product, patenting is not always the best business decision; however, we wanted you to be aware of the rules around public disclosure.

8. **ASK PEERS.** Identify other people in your business community that you think may have insights into the market. Share what you have learned and get their thoughts. Ideally, some of these people will be in the retail industry. You will be amazed by what you will learn by first studying this information and then speaking to others who will also have insights to share. **Note:** If you do your homework before you speak to your peers, your conversations will inevitably be deeper and oftentimes more fruitful. When people see that you are working hard and that you are focused and serious, they tend to be more generous with their time and resources.

In the following chart, let's revisit the TP Saver example. We started with four rings and then sliced the diagram into four markets although we focused on only one market. In the outermost ring, start with the total addressable market. In our case, we know that in the United States there are just over four million babies born each year. Based on discussions with parents, we know that kids tend to pull the toilet paper from the ages of one to two years old, which means there are about eight million kids in this age range. Assuming some households have two kids in this range, the household number is between four million and eight million; we will estimate six million. So, in the outermost ring we will put six million. Next, we need to ask of this number of potential households, how many will actually experience this problem? (See chart on the next page.)

*Large consumer product companies spend a tremendous amount of money on surveys, focus groups, and other research to find out how many people experience the problem their product addresses. (You will learn how to do this in Step 3.) As discussed previously, you can also do this to understand what percentage of people in this demographic experience this problem. Let's say that we learned from our surveys or interviews that one out of four families experienced this problem; we would then write 1.5 million (6 million x 25%) in the second ring. **(Remember this rule of thumb: If you don't know what a customer thinks, don't assume or guess. Ask them.)***

TP Saver Example

Product Target Markets

Market 1: Juvenile $7bn Category

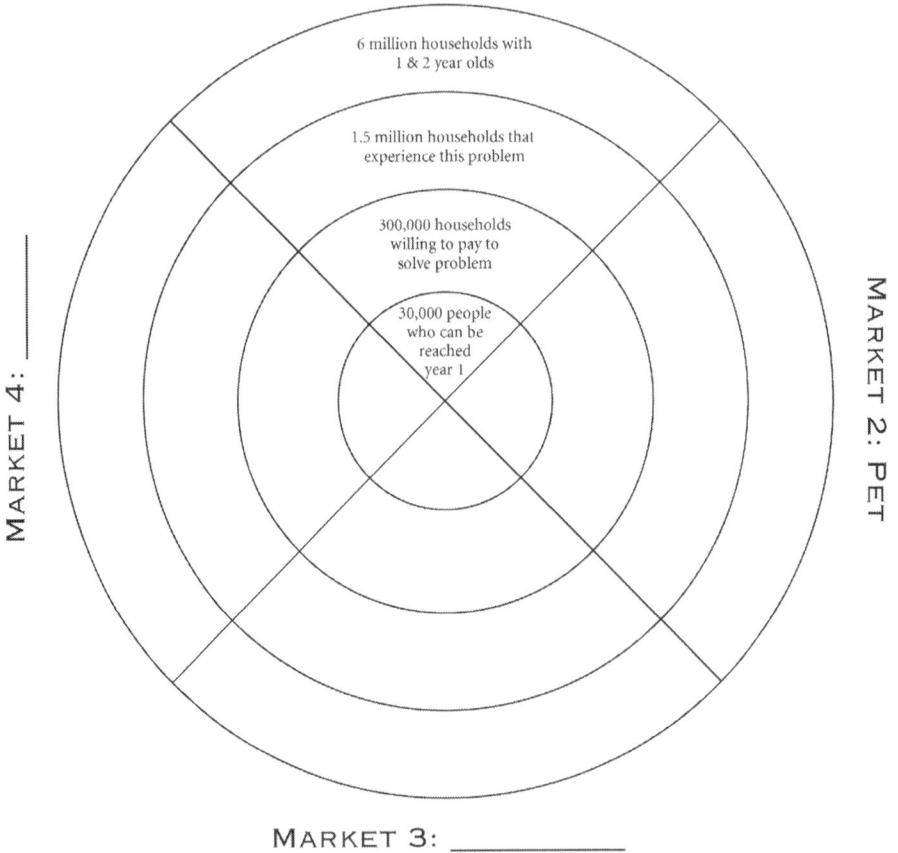

6 million households with
1 & 2 year olds

1.5 million households that
experience this problem

300,000 households
willing to pay to
solve problem

30,000 people
who can be
reached
year 1

Market 4: _____

Market 2: Pet

Market 3: _____

Next, you need to determine of those who experience the problem, how many have enough "pain" or "frustration" associated with this problem that they will purchase a product to fix it. Again, survey data, target customer interviews, and assumptions will be used to further narrow this down. From our interviews, we know that approximately 20 percent of this number would pay to address this problem, so in the third ring we would write 300,000 (1.5 million x 20%). Finally, in the center, we need to estimate how many of these potential consumers we could realistically reach.

Because this is a fairly targeted market and there is no other similar product on the market, we think that it is plausible we could conservatively reach 10 percent of this market (which is a very large market share for a small, new company). This represents 30,000 (300,000 x 10%) families. As you can see, the center of our target is now 30,000 sales. At $1.50 per unit (our initial price estimates were higher than we found would work in the end), that is only $45,000 in total gross revenue.

What this means is that making this product is **not** going to be justified unless (a) our assumptions are too low, or (b) we find other markets to sell into, such as the pet market. Even if we doubled our market share to 20 percent, the total is just $90,000. On the other hand, if we had a different product that generated, say $20 in gross margin per sale (30,000 units x $20 = $600,000 gross revenue), this could be a lucrative market.

Visit TamaraMonosoff.com/guides for a free copy of **"Power Pricing: Demystifying Profit Margins and Mark-ups."** This is a glossary of terms.

In the sample circle graph using the TP Saver market findings, we learned that:

Even though the numbers appeared to show there <u>was</u> a sufficient target market (parents with toddlers), when we dug deeper we found that the number was actually too low. Way too low! The number of toddlers that pulled the toilet paper was too small; the number of parents willing to purchase a product to address the problem was minimal; and the likelihood of reaching that narrow slice of the market was too big of a challenge.

Often, when people do market research, they stop after finding the answer to #1. They say "Oh, good! There are six million households with toddlers, which is plenty of people to buy my product." As you can see, this general data doesn't provide a realistic picture.

In this example, we would go through the same exercise for each relevant market where we might sell our product (recognizing that each distinct market typically requires additional costs such as packaging, marketing, sales, staffing, and knowledge). Then we add up the numbers for each market in the center.

Here's another example of how to gather "big picture" market data. Let's say we want to seek data about lunch box sales. The amount of useful data and the number of additional resources we found in less than 15 minutes of research was surprising.

We first typed "lunch box statistics" and "lunch box sales" into Google. All we found were listings of companies offering lunch boxes for sale. But when we typed **"lunch box"** + **"sales data"** we found some useful information.

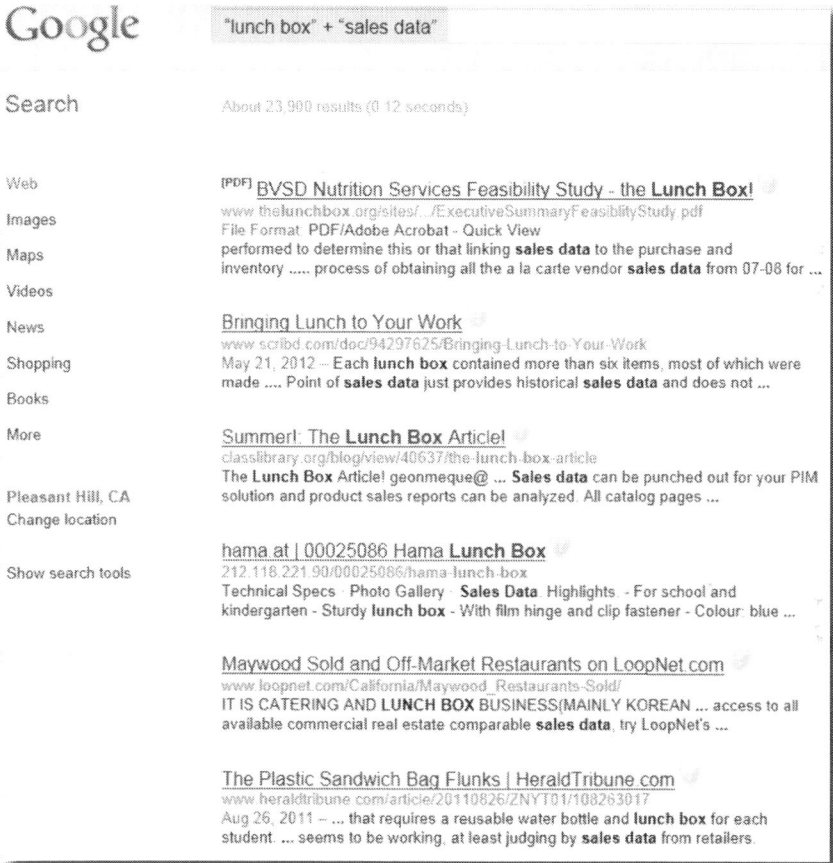

Google   "lunch box" + "sales data"

Search   About 23,900 results (0.12 seconds)

Web

Images

Maps

Videos

News

Shopping

Books

More

Pleasant Hill, CA
Change location

Show search tools

[PDF] BVSD Nutrition Services Feasibility Study - the **Lunch Box**!
www.thelunchbox.org/sites/.../ExecutiveSummaryFeasiblityStudy.pdf
File Format: PDF/Adobe Acrobat - Quick View
performed to determine this or that linking **sales data** to the purchase and
inventory ..... process of obtaining all the a la carte vendor **sales data** from 07-08 for ...

Bringing Lunch to Your Work
www.scribd.com/doc/94297625/Bringing-Lunch-to-Your-Work
May 21, 2012 -- Each **lunch box** contained more than six items, most of which were
made .... Point of **sales data** just provides historical **sales data** and does not ...

Summer!: The **Lunch Box** Article!
classlibrary.org/blog/view/40637/the-lunch-box-article
The **Lunch Box** Article! geonmeque@ ... **Sales data** can be punched out for your PIM
solution and product sales reports can be analyzed. All catalog pages ...

hama.at | 00025086 Hama **Lunch Box**
212.118.221.90/00025086/hama-lunch-box
Technical Specs · Photo Gallery · **Sales Data** · Highlights. - For school and
kindergarten - Sturdy **lunch box** - With film hinge and clip fastener - Colour: blue ...

Maywood Sold and Off-Market Restaurants on LoopNet.com
www.loopnet.com/California/Maywood_Restaurants-Sold/
IT IS CATERING AND **LUNCH BOX** BUSINESS(MAINLY KOREAN ... access to all
available commercial real estate comparable **sales data**, try LoopNet's ...

The Plastic Sandwich Bag Flunks | HeraldTribune.com
www.heraldtribune.com/article/20110826/ZNYT01/108263017
Aug 26, 2011 -- ... that requires a reusable water bottle and **lunch box** for each
student. ... seems to be working, at least judging by **sales data** from retailers.

When you do this, read the various articles, starting with those that are first or appear most relevant. Even if the links are not exactly what you are seeking, be sure to scan these different resources as they will often provide data that is pertinent to your market and will reference sources you may want to look at directly. As we went through the links, at first we did not find anything. Then we found something interesting. At the bottom of the first page of our Google search, there was an article whose headline did not actually appear to be directly relevant. However, we got a pleasant surprise.

We learned directly which lunch box item sales are growing, which are not, and some predictions regarding future trends.

The Plastic Sandwich Bag Flunks

STEPHANIE CLIFFORD

Published: Friday, August 26, 2011 at 11:04 p.m.
Last Modified: Friday, August 26, 2011 at 11:04 p.m.

Many retailers and schools are advocating waste-free options for back-to-school shoppers this year, especially when it comes to lunch. School lists call for Tupperware instead of Ziplocs, neoprene lunch bags instead of brown paper ones, and aluminum water bottles, not the throwaway plastic versions.

Sales of environmentally friendly back-to-school products are up just about everywhere. At the Container Store, the increase is 30 percent over last year for some items, said Mona Williams, the company's vice president of buying. "We have seen a huge resurgence," she said.

The trend makes the schools happy (much less garbage). It makes the stores happy (higher back-to-school spending). It even makes the students happy (green feels good).

Who's not happy? The parents (what to do when the Tupperware runs out?).

"Ziplocs are the biggest misstep," said Julie Corbett, a mother in Oakland, Calif., whose two girls attend a school with an eco-friendly lunch policy. In school years past, she said, many a morning came unhinged when the girls were sent to school with disposable sandwich bags.

Later in the same article additional we found data describing a very important sales trend, making it clear what kinds of products in this category we definitely do NOT want to sell.

Despite the difficulties, the push for eco-friendly products in school lunches seems to be working, at least judging by sales data from retailers.

Sales of paper bags and sandwich bags, which once were school lunch must-haves, are declining. Between August 2010 and August 2011, unit sales of plastic sandwich bags sold declined by 3.17 percent, while paper bags fell by 13.19 percent, compared with the same period a year earlier, according to the market research firm SymphonyIRI Group.

At the Container Store, popular items this year include Japanese bento-box-style lunch boxes, Bobble water bottles with built-in filters, reusable cotton sandwich bags called snackTaxis, and PeopleTowels, machine-washable napkins.

HELPFUL HINT: FOLLOWING BREADCRUMBS

You may have noticed in the article above that you just learned the name of the vice president of buying (Mona Williams) at the Container Store! Make note of this in your Companion Workbook. Buyers come and go, but now you have a starting point when you contact their corporate office if you decide to manufacture and sell your product(s) to retailers. Go to zoominfo.com to get the Container Store corporate office contact information, which is not readily available on their website. However, after a one-minute search at ContainerStore.com, at the bottom of their homepage in small print, you'll find "contact." When you click "contact," you'll see one option they give you is to present your product to the Container Store via: newproducts@containerstore.com. The point here is not to get sidetracked but to pay attention to the other surprising gifts you discover when you're doing your market research. Just make note of them in an organized way as this information may come in handy later.

Next, we changed the search words to "Lunch Box" + "Statistics" which lead to:

A New Twist on Lunch: A Bento Box for Better Health | The Friedman...
friedmansprout.com/.../a-new-twist-on-lunch-a-bento-box-for-better-...
Mar 29, 2010 – **Lunch-box** nutrition never looked so good! Susan Yuen packs 2 ....
Center for Disease Control, National Center for Health **Statistics**.

While we still did not get the entire answer we were seeking, we did find a few more pieces to our jigsaw puzzle with the following data:

With nearly 20% of American children ages 6-11 classified as overweight, there has been closer scrutiny of school lunch nutrition standards. Nearly all public schools participate in the government subsidized National School Lunch Program (NSLP), which provides 30.5 million lunches to children every day. Lunches are based on the 2005 Dietary Guidelines for Americans, but compliance is not always perfect.

Do not leave possible gemstones uncovered in your digging! Whenever you find useful data, read the author's source data and then take time to go there. There could be information in that data that was not included in their article. Below is the list of resources for this article on school lunch trends that would be worth digging into as well.

Sources

2005 Dietary Guidelines for Americans.
http://www.cnpp.usda.gov/Publications/DietaryGuidelines/2005/2005DGPolic

"Bento Basics." Just Bento. http://justbento.com/handbook/bento-basics

Center for Disease Control, National Center for Health Statistics.
http://www.cdc.gov/HealthyYouth/obesity/

Chen, Sheri. Email correspondence. March 12th, 2010.

Clark MA, Fox MK. Nutritional quality of the diets of US public school children and the role of the school meal programs. JAMA. 2009 Feb; 109(2):S44-56.

Crepinsek MK, Gordon AR, McKinney PM, Condon EM, Wilson A. Meals offered and served in US public schools: do they meet nutrient standards? Journal of the American Dietetic Association. 2009 Feb;109(2):S31-43.

Ekuan, Kenji. The Aesthetics of the Japanese Lunchbox. The MIT Press: Cambridge. 2000, Pg. 188.

Miura-Kaminaka, M. The Japanese Cultural Center of Hawaii. The Legacy of the Japanese in Hawai'i: Cuisine. Fisher Printing Co, Inc. 1989.

MyPyramid for Kids. United States Department of Agriculture.
http://teamnutrition.usda.gov/Resources/mpk_poster2.pdf

National School Lunch Program Fact Sheet. USDA Food and Nutrition Service.
http://www.fns.usda.gov/cnd/Lunch/AboutLunch/NSLPFactSheet.pdf

We used this lunch box example to show you (as we did with the TP Saver) how to gather the big picture market data and trend information. After you have rigorously done all of this research and followed every new information trail as far as possible, you will be far more knowledgeable than when you began. At some point the science of studying the true value of your product, the existing market data, and the views and feedback of your target customers and business peers becomes an art. In other words, there comes a point when you use your own insights and the insights of others to frame an opinion that is as realistic as possible as to the market potential of your product.

Pulling Together the Market Data

Using the data you have gathered so far, do your best to quantify your markets. Write your findings on the chart on the next page, "Product Target Markets." Remember to put the big picture market numbers in the space on the chart that is the farthest from the center. As you refine your market size, you move closer to the bull's-eye (center of chart). The information inside the bull's-eye will be the most specific and realistic estimate of the number of people you will target to purchase your product.

PRODUCT NAME: _____

PRODUCT TARGET MARKETS

MARKET 1: _____

MARKET 4: _____

MARKET 2: _____

MARKET 3: _____

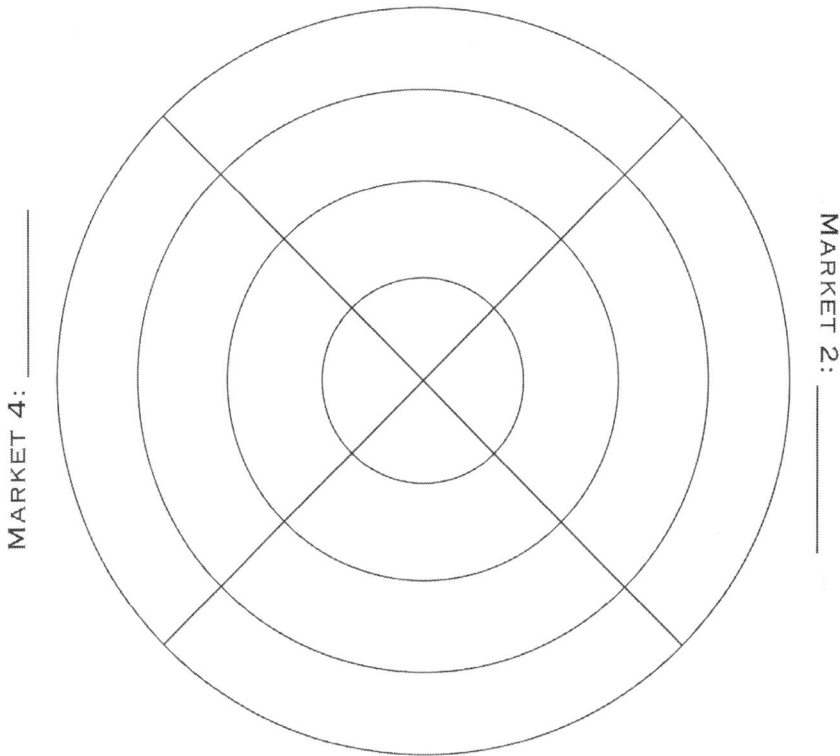

RANK THE VIABILITY AND POTENTIAL OF
YOUR REALISTIC TARGET MARKET

1	2	3
SMALL MARKET		LARGE MARKET

In the next section (Step 3), we will teach you how to get feedback and valuable customer insights about your product. You will need this information to complete the chart above.

If you are feeling overwhelmed right now, please don't worry. As with doing anything worthwhile, it takes patience and stamina. If you follow the steps to the end of this book, all the pieces of the puzzle will come together.

Keep going!

STEP 3: FEEDBACK: WHAT DO PEOPLE HONESTLY THINK ABOUT YOUR PRODUCT?

> **The purpose of this section is to enable you to determine what benefits your product will deliver and how consumers will respond to your product.**

The reality is that the consumer market is fickle. People must see meaningful value when changing behavior or trying new products. The best way to answer this BIG question about the targetable market for your specific product is to gather outside evidence and information.

How much people are willing to pay for a product (or service) depends on how much they need or want it. We liken this to the comparison of buying medicine or vitamins. People will spend almost any amount, at any time—irrespective of marketing—on medicine that will cure them. They "need" it. On the other hand, vitamins could be useful, but the "need" is not self-evident without a tremendous amount of information and marketing persuasion.

The fashion industry is a good example of marketing persuasion. Women don't necessarily "need" to have the latest (handbags, sweater, etc.), but fashion companies spend millions of dollars on marketing to create that emotional "need." In other words, their goal is to convert the "want" to "need," often marketing to your emotions. They will show you that by having their sweater, you will "feel" more beautiful, sexy, hip … which will help improve your self-esteem and how you "feel" about yourself. Therefore, wearing their sweater will make you more desirable and successful in your life. The goal is to get you to the point where you feel you "need" to have that sweater, rather than feeling it's something that would be "nice to have."

4 Key Questions to Ask and Answer in the Process of Gathering this Data:

- ✓ What problem is this product solving for consumers?
- ✓ What are the specific complaints online and in the market about the problem and how common are they?
- ✓ How much money is saved by using your product?
- ✓ Does your product fall into the "need" category or is it a "nice to have"?

In this section we are going to help you answer these questions by using non-empirical data (opinions) and empirical data (statistics and metrics). Throughout this process you will want to document:

1. The methods used to gather data (surveys, etc.)
2. The process used for quantifying data (How did you tabulate the information?)
3. The breakdown of the results (summarize your findings)

The first step you will take is to:
- ✓ Search Google or Bing and type in the phrases:
  - o "complaint about (problem your product solves)"
  - o "blog about (subject area of your product)"
  - o "solution for (the problem your product solves)"
  - o "reviews on (the issue your product addresses)"

> **TIP:** If you find highly relevant websites and statistics, be sure to bookmark them for future reference and note them in your Companion Workbook.

The second step will be to select other methods for gathering data. These could include informal focus groups, street interviews, e-mail blasts, or online surveys.

Each of these methods will require five things:
1. Preplanned questions
2. The identification of target subjects
3. A method for engaging subjects
4. A method for capturing data
5. A method for analyzing the data

When you are planning your questions, keep in mind that you will want to get data that can be tabulated as well as input that is less structured. You cannot expect people to spend too much time, so you want to limit your questions. You can, however, make each question address both requirements by asking them in two parts.

For example:
1. **Do you find that ___ is a problem you struggle with?**
   The benefit of asking the question in this way is that in the results you can say, "X out of 20 people interviewed said 'Yes.'"

2. **How do you deal with this issue today?**
   This question provides a chance to get more subjective and descriptive feedback.

Informal Focus Groups

Convening an informal focus group involves getting a group of people together who will share their feedback in a comfortable environment where answers can be clarified and discussed.

- There are many different ways to host informal focus group meetings. First, plan the get-together or series of group meetings with friends and acquaintances that represent your target market and ask each participant to bring someone you don't know. It's usually best not to hold these meetings in your home (maybe have a friend host the meeting) as the participants may not feel as if they can be candid with their answers because they are a guest in your home. Therefore, you may wish to tap into a group to which you belong for participants (e.g., mommy's group, religious group, or club). You may also be able to get some time on the agenda within an existing group meeting. In addition, local libraries and civic or community centers will oftentimes rent rooms at a reasonable rate.

- Tell your participants that you value their feedback, both positive and negative. Let them know that you want them to be truthful and that you see negative feedback as a gift because it will help you understand if it makes sense to develop the product.

- Have the participants sign a release form that states they will keep the group discussion and product information shared confidential. (Sometimes verbal agreement is all you can get. Just document the date and time that this discussion occurred in your Companion Workbook.)

(Go to www.TamaraMonosoff.com/Guides for a free Release Form.)

- List the questions you plan to ask and listen to the responses carefully. Not only will you have the opportunity to get specific feedback about the product, but you may even hear great ideas for future additions to your product line.

- Ask one person to take notes for you or ask permission to tape or videotape the session. (Go to www.TamaraMonosoff.com/Guides for a free Permission to Tape or Videotape form.)

- Ask another person to ask the questions (below) and lead the discussion so that you are free to listen.

- Ask everyone in the group to provide an e-mail address (have them sign a sheet before they leave) so that you can send follow-up questions and a special thank you. Sometimes inventors provide a $25-$100 gift card to some general, well-traveled, or online store (e.g., Target, Amazon) as a gift for their efforts.

Street Interviews or Intercepts
By stopping people in their tracks (called intercepts) and quickly interviewing them about your product, you can get immediate feedback. These kinds of interviews are informal, and they can help you focus on key issues to help refine your product design.

- Choose a public place (e.g., supermarket, mall, street, post office, park, wherever your target market spends time).

- When you stop people to interview, be sure to identify yourself immediately, speak warmly, and concisely explain what you are doing. *"Hi. My name is Sarah and I'm developing a new pet product that makes it easier to groom your dog. Do you have a dog? I want to avoid making mistakes. May I ask you a few questions to get your feedback about the product?"* Make sure your eagerness doesn't come across as aggressiveness and ask them for permission to ask them a few quick questions. Tell them that their answers will be anonymous. Don't ask them for their contact information. If they say "No," be gracious, thank them, and move on to the next person. Interview as many people as possible.

- Rehearse your approach and questions so that you don't sound disorganized.

- If you want them to fill something out, have a few questions pre-printed on a form with a clipboard. People are busy, so it may be more effective for you to ask them the questions and then quickly jot down the answers yourself.

E-mail Blasts

E-mail is a powerful way to collect information. Create an e-mail campaign and send it to your network of family, friends, and business associates.

- Send out a brief message with a request for information. Let them know you are gathering market information about a product you are developing and that you need feedback from people who are experiencing the problem your product solves. Describe the consumer or target you are looking to speak with. (For example, "If you know any

women currently planning a wedding, please forward.")
Then include your questions in the actual body of the e-mail
message so that it is easy for people to respond. In other
words, don't send an attached document. Mention your
deadline and, most importantly, express your gratitude for
their help.

Online Feedback

Another quick and effective way to get information about
your product is to post questions in online forums where you
find your target customers spending time. However, make
sure to be mindful of the rules and etiquette of the forum.
Don't try to "sell" anything or you will be quickly ousted from
the group. The goal here is to ask questions and to carefully
listen to people's thoughts and opinions.

Conduct an Online Survey

There are great online survey tools available today that you
can use to gather information about your product. With these
tools, you can prepare surveys in minutes without any
technical know-how. The survey tool platforms below will
prompt you through the process, and at the end they will
generate a link that you can e-mail or blast out via your blogs
and social media networks to generate responses.

Here are just a few:

o www.SurveyMonkey.com – the most well-known online
  survey tool for easily collecting and analyzing data
o www.PopSurvey.com – a simple online survey tool with
  beautiful templates that's easy to use
o www.FormStack.com is not a survey tool; however, you
  can use it to create interactive forms to gather
  information that can be used like a survey. One thing I
  like about FormStack.com is that respondents are able to

attach pictures and videos to their forms. Although you can gather information in an organized way using FormStack.com, it does not offer survey analysis as do the other tools mentioned above.

Here are some sample questions to get you started from *The Mom Inventors Handbook* (page 83) to ask about your product. You can use these questions or variations of these questions that are specific to your product for any of the methods of gathering data mentioned above.

- o Have you seen anything like it before?
- o How have you dealt with this issue without this product?
- o Would you purchase this product? How many?
- o If not, why not?
- o What do you like about it?
- o What would you change?
- o What colors would you prefer?
- o How much would you pay for it?
- o Where would you expect to buy it? (Name specific stores where you shop.)
- o How would you expect it to be packaged?
- o How many per package?

Although these questions are designed to help you get started gathering information about your product, there are a number of ways to "ask" your potential customers for information. One goal when going through this process is to figure out how to deepen your questions. In other words, you might ask:

- o Financial questions: "How much would you pay for this product?" Then ask the opposite question, "What price would be too high to pay for this product?"

o   Questions that describe the needs of your customers: "Describe any issues you face daily, weekly, or monthly that relate to [describe the need your product addresses]." "How big of an issue is this for you?" "How have you dealt with this problem in the past?" "Have you discussed this issue with friends and family?"

Even though research data is often deemed more reliable, we value what people tell us (interviews, surveys, etc.), and we think that gathering both kinds of information is the best way to understand your market.

We have shown you how to get started gathering direct data about your product (above) on your own without spending a lot of money. However, if you feel that you need additional support conducting online or in-person surveys and interviews, there are market research firms that you can hire that will work with you to gather the information you are seeking about your target market (i.e. consumers who will buy your product). This can get pricy; however, there are boutique firms that cater to small business owners such as www.SilverStork.com and www.amplifyresearch.com/. They both are Mom-Owned Businesses that we know personally.

Be sure to write detailed notes about your direct market research results in your Companion Workbook.

INDUSTRY DATA

Carefully gathering empirical industry research data is a valuable step for forming the basis for moving forward with your product. The reliability and accuracy of source data is critical. It is often also the hardest to find.

When developing data, you will first look for specific data already produced. Technology companies often use published report data about money spent on a given problem. So first look for this kind of data using search engines and industry sources. Many industry publications (e.g., *Kids Today*—juvenile sector) can provide a wealth of information. Many industry groups sponsor and publish specific research data. Some examples are:

- The Juvenile Products Manufacturing Association (http://www.jpma.org)
- The International Housewares Association (http:///www.housewares.org)
- The American Pet Products Association (http://www.americanpetproducts.org/)
- Direct Selling Association (http://www.dsa.org/)

Sometimes you hit the jackpot and find exactly what you are looking for. Other times, you need to pull together more disconnected data, especially if your product is very new and innovative.

Use a search engine (e.g., Google or Yahoo) and search variations on the "problem that your product solves + statistics" or your product type or the actual industry. For example, if we were developing a new type of yoga accessory, we would need to understand the yoga market. (See search examples below.) It took only two clicks to find incredible yoga industry data using "yoga statistics." It can be exciting when you find something after making a subtle change to your search description.

Yoga Statistics
f Share on Facebook

We found this great market data (below) by searching "Yoga Statistics"

Statistic Verification
Source: NAMASTA, YIAS, LiveStrong, Yoga Journal
Date Verified: 7.2.2012

From this single search, look at the other great resources we found! NAMASTA, Yoga Journal, etc. offer more detailed statistics. Read their Press Releases.

Yoga Demographics and Statistics	
Total Number of Americans who practice Yoga	15 million
Percent female	72.2%
Percent male	27.8%
Precent who earn more than $75,000 annually	44%
Percent who earn more than $100,000 annually	24%
Percent between the ages of 18-34	40.6%
Percent between the ages of 35-54	41%
Percent over 55	18.4%
Percent who are college graduates	71.4%
Yoga by Location	
Percent of practitioners that live on the West Coast	20 %
Percent of practitioners that live in the Northeast	30 %
Percent of practitioners that live in the Midwest including Ohio	30 %
Other parts	20 %
Yoga Industry Growth Statistics	
Amount spent annually in the US on yoga products	$27 Billion
Percent increase on yoga product spending over the last 5 years	87 %
Average annual increase of the number of people who practice yoga	20 %

Personal Market Research Data Log: (Write your notes here)

_____

_____

_____

Not only did we find great data from a single search under "yoga statistics" but we also found additional resources like *Yoga Journal* that offer even more detailed market research to help you get a broader understanding of the yoga market.

Other sources that can increase your knowledge about the benefits associated with your product are blogs and posts from relevant communities. Plus, you can make posts to relevant communities yourself. For example, if you were working on a yoga product, using search engines, you would find relevant blogs and communities. If they have search windows on their sites, search on the need your product solves. If you see nothing, create a post and see what you hear in response. For example, if you were developing a new yoga mat that had arm extensions, write a post that says, "Does anyone else have an issue with your arms coming off the yoga mat? If so, how do you address it?" Write the same kind of post on sites that are not as industry specific but that reach your demographic. For example, if it is a product for women, create posts on a mom blog like www.CafeMom.com or on a women's forum like Yahoo's Shine http://shine.yahoo.com.

Using this method, you may be able to produce your own empirical data. To do so, it is necessary to quantify the cost (in money, time, or other measurement) of using a current product or process without the benefit of your new product. Then you need to mathematically show the savings achieved by using your product.

We will use Tamara's first invention, the TP Saver®, as an example.

Let's say that toilet paper costs about $1 per roll. When a toddler or pet discovers the fun of unraveling the toilet paper, they can unravel a roll a day. Even with effort, parents have reported a loss of five rolls in a single bathroom in a week for six months. In just one month that is $20 (and $120 over six months) in lost toilet paper costs, not accounting for the headache. At a cost of $1.50/unit price for the TP Saver, you would save $118.50 over a six-month period. You might also have the associated cost of hiring a plumber or fixing flood-damaged floors resulting from clogged toilets caused by kids stuffing too much toilet paper down the toilet.

This data can then be combined with other empirical statistics and with the non-empirical data gathered via surveys, informal focus groups, etc. to give reliable insights into the true benefit of your product.

The claim you make based on your research should clearly identify your product's value, utility, and benefits. For example, it might say something to the effect of: "This new (product name) will (do something important). For example, this new reusable bag will eliminate the use of 380 billion plastic bags used by Americans per year at a cost savings of (amount of money saved $X). Further, we know that people will prefer (product name) because we have surveyed 360 potential customers and personally conducted 20 extended one-on-one interviews with potential customers."

The clearest evaluation of "utility" or usefulness is when both empirical and non-empirical data are shown to support the case for value. Unfortunately, even the most diligent inventors often stop their research at this point and base their decisions on data they have gathered thus far.

As I mentioned before, with the cost savings data we just outlined, the TP Saver seems like a very compelling product. In addition, the focus groups we conducted also gave positive data. However, as we previously illustrated in Step 2, the potential market size and per-unit profit turned out to be too small to make the TP Saver a sufficiently successful product.

The key to your efforts here will be to combine this industry data with the market data (steps 2 and 3) and profit potential (steps 7 and 10) to complete the financial picture. Do your best to finish this section, but know that it is still too early to make a decision.

Can you make new assertions as to the true need and benefits your product will deliver?

_____

_____

_____

_____

_____

BASED ON WHAT YOU HAVE LEARNED IN THIS SECTION, RANK THE MARKET STRENGTH (SIZE, INDUSTRY, SURVEY FEEDBACK) OF YOUR PRODUCT.

1	2	3
LOW USEFULNESS		HIGHLY USEFUL

We just had you look carefully at the need for your product and its true usefulness. In the next section, we show you how to research the existing patents and trademarks related to your product.

STEP 4: LEGAL: HOW CAN YOU SEARCH OTHER PATENTS & TRADEMARKS TO GET FREE LEGAL INSIGHTS?

The purpose of this section is to teach you how to research existing patents and trademarks related to your product.

This section is not intended to teach you how to write a patent or a trademark, or even guide you in making the decision to file any intellectual property. However, the subject is important to this process for two main reasons:

First, it is important to be aware of the patents that already exist that are either identical or related to your product. This way you can determine whether your product, as it is currently conceived, may or may not infringe on the patent rights owned by others.

Second, it will help you evaluate whether you have the potential to file your own patent should you choose to do so, and to factor this possibility into your overall product analysis.

Why do I need to research patents and trademarks?
1. To understand existing IP (intellectual property)
2. To avoid infringing on someone else's patent/trademarks
3. To get free legal advice to save money

BASIC LEGAL DEFINITIONS

Before we dive into this section, we want to define a few terms for you. For the most part, we simply used Wikipedia definitions as they are relatively straightforward. We did add some content where we thought it was necessary to simplify or expand the definitions:

Intellectual Property (IP)
"Creations of the mind..." For our purposes, when we say "intellectual property" or "IP," we are referring to patents, trademarks and copyright filings with the www.USPTO.gov.

Invention
A unique or novel device, method, composition, or process. It may be an improvement upon a machine or product, or a new process for creating an object or a result. An invention that achieves a completely unique function or result may be a radical breakthrough. Such works are novel and not obvious to others skilled in the same field. *Wikipedia*

Patent
A patent is a form of intellectual property. It consists of a set of exclusive rights granted by a sovereign state to an inventor or their assignee for a limited period of time, in exchange for the public disclosure of the invention. *Wikipedia*

There are different kinds of patents.
The two that are most common in our experience are utility patents and design patents.

- A utility patent is the patent considered the most valuable—and difficult to receive. This patent addresses the way something is done. For example, it could be the way in which something is attached or how something is achieved using this invention.

- A design patent, on the other hand, is very specifically the actual design of something. So, absent a utility patent, there could be multiple products that do the same thing but only one with the exact design as the one holding a design patent. Because designs can vary, this design patent is much less useful, as a competitor merely must modify their design modestly to avoid infringement.

Novelty

Novelty is a patentability requirement. An invention is not patentable if the claimed subject matter was disclosed before the date of filing or before the date of priority (if a priority is claimed) of the patent application. *Wikipedia*

Prior Art

Prior art constitutes all information that has been made available to the public in any form before a given date that might be relevant to a patent's claims of originality. If an invention has been described in the prior art, a patent on that invention is not valid. *Wikipedia*

A Novelty Search (also known as a Patent Search)

A "novelty search" is a prior art search that is often conducted by patent attorneys, patent agents, or professional patent searchers before an inventor files a patent application. A novelty search helps an inventor determine if the invention is novel before the inventor commits the resources necessary to obtain a patent. *Wikipedia*

Provisional Patent Application (PPA)

Under United States patent law, a provisional application is a legal document filed in the United States Patent and Trademark Office (USPTO) that establishes an early filing date, but which does not mature into an issued patent unless the applicant files a regular non-provisional patent application within one year. There is no such thing as a "provisional patent." *Wikipedia*

Disclaimer: We are not attorneys and do not provide legal advice or opinions. None of this information should be used by itself to make decisions about legal issues related to your product. Consult a qualified attorney for legal advice.

While it is unlikely that someone without legal training will be able to render a legally certified opinion as to whether their product will infringe on an existing similar item, or if it is patentable, it is absolutely possible to form an understanding of what else has been claimed and filed and how extensive the filings have been for a particular invention type. Reading as many similar or associated patents as possible is the best way to achieve this.

You will be amazed at how much you learn by reading related patent documents. In effect, you will give yourself hundreds of dollars worth of free legal advice because the opinions have been written by patent attorneys who have drafted patent filings that have been successfully granted.

Historically, patent rights in the United States were based on the "first to invent." This meant that an American inventor could keep his or her documented proof that he or she "invented" a product first, even if someone else filed a patent on it first. On March 16, 2013, new provisions to U.S. patent law, known as "first-to-file," went into effect. The implications of this change are broad and include alignment with the rest of the world, reduced fees for some, and increased difficulty in obtaining a patent. The key change is that the patent rights will now be granted to the first person to both conceive of *and* to reduce the invention to practice by filing a patent first. We still recommend maintaining records of "conception" of your invention. (We have provided these pages for you in the Companion Workbook.) And we do not believe this means every inventor should rush out and file a patent. However, if a patent or provisional application is something you plan to file, be aware of this change to the provisions to U.S. patent law. Consult your attorney for legal advice.

10 Tips to Make Your Patent Research Easier:

These 10 Tips are the key elements of this section with Tips 1-6 providing basic knowledge of the search tools and Tips 7-10 requiring deeper digging, reading, printing, and note-taking.

Patents can be found at:
- U.S. Patent & Trademark Office (http://www.uspto.gov)
- Google Patents (http://www.google.com/patents/)
- Patent Storm (http://www.patentstorm.com)
- Patent Genius (http://www.patentgenius.com)
- Free Patents Online (http://www.freepatentsonline.com)

The following steps will show you how we use these sites and what we look for: (Go to www.TamaraMonosoff.com/Guides to see a video tutorial.)

1. When using patent search sites such as those mentioned above, there is usually a search window. In this search window, type in the most descriptive word(s) possible including the "function" of your product (i.e., what it does) to help you get started. Our preference is Google Patents as we have found it the easiest to use. For example, when we go to http://www.google.com/patents and type in "garden trowel," a large number of patents are listed.

2. Once you find patents for items that are similar, you will see that most of these sites offer an image of the patent filing and an option to read the text. **Look at the photo first**. We click on the images as we find it easier to determine how closely related this patent is to our idea by first viewing an image.

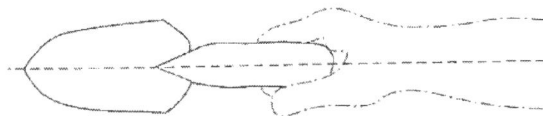

Fig - 3

3. Look at the patent number and figure out if it is a "utility" or "design" patent. If a "D" is the first character in the patent number, it is a design patent. This is usually good news for you.

A design patent is the weakest form of patent because it protects only the precise design of the product. A utility patent is much more powerful. It covers the function, task, or process the product achieves. In the example above, there is not a "D" listed in the patent number, which means it is a "utility" patent.

4. Look at the "Date Issued." If it was issued more than 20 years ago, you know that this patent is now expired. This is good news and bad news. Good because it is not owned by someone else and you can use it. Bad because it is now in the public domain and therefore not something to which you can likely claim patent rights.

(12) **United States Design Patent**   (10) Patent No.:   **US D504,889 S**
Andre et al.   (45) **Date of Patent:**   ** **May 10, 2005**

(54) **ELECTRONIC DEVICE**

(75) Inventors: Bartley K. Andre, Menlo Park, CA (US), Daniel J. Coster, San Francisco, CA (US); Daniele De Iuliis, San Francisco, CA (US), Richard P. Howarth, San Francisco, CA (US); Jonathan P. Ive, San Francisco, CA (US); Steve Jobs, Palo Alto, CA (US);

D396,452 S   *   7/1998   Naruki D14/424
D451,505 S   *   12/2001   Iseki et al D14/341
D453,333 S   *   2/2002   Chen D14/374
D458,252 S   *   6/2002   Palm et al. D14/343

OTHER PUBLICATIONS

Andre et al., U.S. Appl. No. 29/180,558 entitled "Electronic Device", filed Mar. 17, 2004.
"HP Compaq Tablet PC tc1100", downloaded Aug. 27,

Find Date Issued Here.

5. Download necessary third-party viewing tools such as Adobe Reader (http://get.adobe.com/reader/) or another viewer (depending on the site you use) to see the images. NOTE: We have found Google Patents to be the easiest to use as there is no additional download needed.

6. Next, when reading a specific patent, read the section called "Claims." This is the most relevant section of a patent document. This is where you will find the "how" that is the part of the invention to which other people have been granted ownership. Keep in mind that a utility patent is not filed on a "product" but on specific "claims" about that product.

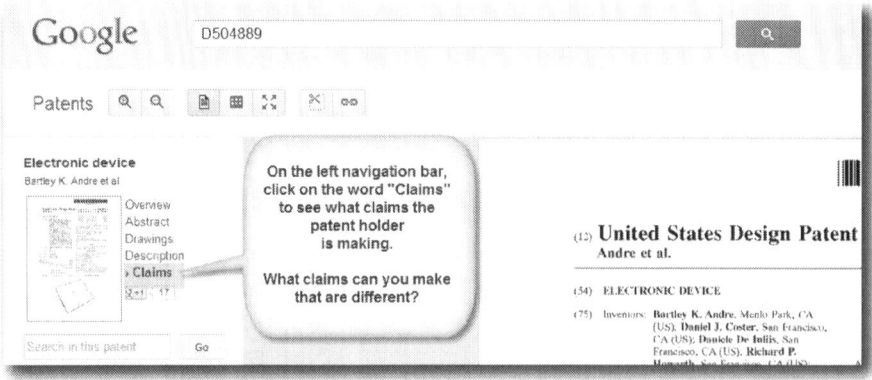

Here's an example that was recently in the news: Apple does not hold the rights to "cell phones," which is evident from the fact that there are many cell phone manufacturers with products available. However, Apple holds numerous patents claiming rights to the way they are "doing or achieving" certain things with the iPhone. So, read the claims of patents that are related to your product. You may need to read a few patents before you find one with claims similar to what you are creating.

Here's another example, using a "gadget" as a product. A patent often does not prevent others from producing their own "gadgets." But if your gadget is fastened using a unique and "novel" way of fastening, your "claim" would enable you to defend your right, should someone attempt to copy your fastening method.

7. When you find a patent that is related to your product, you have discovered the first bread crumb in a trail you will now follow to get closer and closer to the patent(s) in existence that are closest to your invention. Once you find relevant patents, record the patent numbers as you will want to use this process in more than one patent search engine and some may produce different results.

8.   Now we are going to show you how to get free legal advice from dozens of professional patent attorneys. Within each patent filing you will find a section called "Citations" or "Patent References" (or "Field of Search" in some patents that are less detailed). These sections list the other related patents that the attorney or agent who filed the patent you are reading used to show that their filing was unique. As you review this list, click the link or copy and search the patent numbers for the others that appear most closely related to yours. After doing this for a while, you will gain an incredible amount of understanding as to what is out there today and how professionals have written the claims.

9.   As you follow step 8 above, print or note the patents you believe to be closest to your product so that you can save yourself time if you later hire an attorney. You can present your own research, helping expedite the attorney's efforts. You will have a more intelligent and efficient initial consultation because you won't be burning precious time as the attorney explains basic patent concepts to you. This will save you money and earn the respect of your attorney.

> **TIP:** A patent is an asset that costs between $3,000 and $50,000 or more to have drafted and filed depending on the complexity of the product. Since a patent is an asset owned by someone or something (an entity like a company), it can be sold. It has been estimated that over 97 percent of patented inventions never become products. If you find a patent that is precisely your invention, while initially this may feel disappointing, this could actually represent a time-saving opportunity. If you have verified that the inventor has not taken his or her product to market, it may make sense to have an attorney review it. If there is a fit, you could contact the inventor and see if he or she is willing to sell the patent. Many inventors who have been unable to get to market would be delighted to recover some or all of their costs. They would remain the inventor, but you would own the rights to the patent claims. If that is your chosen approach, you can literally save yourself three or more years in this process.

10. There is a temptation to read the summary of the invention and skip the "claims" as these often sound legalistic. Read the claims. These are the keys to the patentability of your invention. Print and highlight those that seem to overlap the most with key aspects of your product idea. From what you learn, you may be able to modify your method to further differentiate your product. (This is the kind of discussion worth having with a creative patent attorney.)

Go to www.TamaraMonosoff.com/Guides to view the patent research video tutorial.

Now that you have dug into existing patents, we want to provide some additional information about patents and the process.

*For a more extensive overview on a technical search, visit http://www.simplepatents.com and view their excellent tutorial.

Caution:

There is a distinct kind of firm out there called an "Invention Promotion Company" that preys on the naïve enthusiasm of inventors. They always "love" your invention, and for an inventor it can be very exciting to meet a businessperson who "gets" their invention. They claim to represent major manufacturers and will do everything for you, starting with an assessment. Then they offer a marketability study that tells you how fabulous your idea is and claim they will find a licensing partner for you. They often claim to have privileged relationships with manufacturers and retailers. Once they lure you in for a few hundred dollars, they will then come back with large fees (e.g., $10,000) to get your product to market. Hundreds of inventors have fallen prey to these companies.

The patent search engines we have recommended above often carry online advertisements for invention promotion companies. (It appears that these companies have even bought key Google search "Ad Words" they associate with Tamara!) Any company that guarantees to get you a patent and makes offers that sound too good to be true should be avoided.

There are very few legitimate firms out there that operate on a contingency basis. That means that they get paid only if they land a deal on your behalf, rather than charge you large fees up-front. However, these firms turn down 99 percent of inventors who approach them as they can afford to represent only a small number of the best items they see.

We do not recommend that you use licensing agents as we believe you are the best advocate for your product. However, if you do go down that path, we recommend you follow these steps:

1. Visit the United States Patent and Trademark Office (http://www.uspto.gov) and in the search box, type "complaints." You will find a list of firms against which people have filed complaints. You will also note the same names appearing again and again (which also often correspond with the big invention advertiser names). The image below is intended to show you where to find this information and is only a partial list of companies. Because of prior complaints, it is not uncommon for these firms to offer their services under several names. Also, it should be noted that these are complaints, not judgments.

2. Visit the Federal Trade Commission website (http://www.ftc.gov) and in the search box, type "invention promotion companies." Read their advice as to what to watch for.

Federal Trade Commission

Facts for Consumers

Email   PDF Format

Invention Promotion Firms

Think you have a great idea for a new product or service? You're not alone. Every year, tens of thousands of people try to develop their ideas and commercially market them.

Some people try to sell their idea or invention to a manufacturer that would market it and pay royalties. But finding a company to do that can be difficult. As an alternative, others use the services of an invention promotion firm. Indeed, some inventors pay thousands of dollars to firms that promise to evaluate, develop, patent, and market inventions... and then do little or nothing for their fees.

Unscrupulous promoters take advantage of an inventor's enthusiasm for a new product or service. They not only urge inventors to patent their ideas or invention, but they also make false and exaggerated claims about the market potential of the invention. The facts are:

- few inventions ever make it to the marketplace; and
- although a patent can provide valuable protection for a successful invention, getting a patent doesn't necessarily increase the chances of commercial success.

There's great satisfaction in developing a new product or service and in getting a patent. But when it comes to determining market potential, inventors should proceed with caution as they try to avoid falling for the sweet-sounding promises of a fraudulent promotion firm.

Using Invention Promotion Firms

Advertisements for invention promotion firms are on television, radio and the Internet, and in newspapers and magazines. These ads target independent inventors with offers of free information on how to patent and market their inventions. Often, however, the only information you get is about the promoter.

If you respond to the ads — which may urge you to call a toll-free number — you may hear back from a salesperson who will ask for a

We have tremendous respect and appreciation for the unique knowledge a patent attorney has and the role he or she plays. Generally we find that their $250 to $400 per hour rates are justified if used properly: for their legal opinions, to draft legal filings, and when necessary to take legal action.

In the early days, prior to pursuing any new product, we always paid an attorney hundreds of dollars to review the existing intellectual property. However, we could have learned a lot on our own first. This section alone will save you that initial $600 to $800 that you might have paid an attorney simply to familiarize you with prior filings. In addition, you will have a greater understanding than if someone else had done it for you. Plus, you will know how to repeat this process in the future.

After you've completed this research, if you do hire an attorney, she will need only to fill in the gaps rather than charge you for her time to do everything, including giving you a basic education.

After you have been through the above steps and the rest of this assessment, you may decide to go forward with a professional patent search. There are legitimate firms that conduct patent searches for a relatively small amount of money. (http://www.walsh-ip.com offers patent searches for $450 or in two steps at $200 each step. http://www.legalzoom.com offers a search for $299.)

A patent attorney will also provide this service and offer opinions as to the patentability of your item. NOTE: They may be outsourcing the search to a firm like SimplePatents.com and marking the cost up. Therefore, going through an attorney is generally more costly but may be worth it because they will then be prepared to take the next step of filing a patent for you if this is ultimately what you decide to do.

Another important thing to understand is that at any given time when you or a professional is conducting research, you are seeing only the patents that have been issued or have been in process within the patent system for some time. There will always be patent applications that are still pending and have not yet been publicized. In addition, provisional patent applications (PPAs) are not made public.

Unfortunately this is a gap in information that is simply not available to the public and presents a bit of a risk. However, while it is a risk, this can be used to your advantage by using the provisional patent application process for yourself, as described below.

The decision to file a patent is often a difficult one. First, most inventions can be granted *some* kind of patent coverage. However, all patents are NOT equal. As stated above, a patent doesn't necessarily cover the "product" but will usually cover some aspect of the product (i.e., the claims).

The value and use of a patent is dependent on what claims are actually covered, how broad they are, and if ownership of those claims is of any benefit. A design patent is extremely limited. Basically, it covers your precise design, which means that it often can be copied with minimal modifications. Therefore, it is much easier to be granted a design patent. The second determinant as to the value of the patent is if anyone else cares to own that right. And third is whether the patent owner has the incentive and financial wherewithal to defend the patent. There are no patent police who are going to tell someone they cannot copy your product. And legally policing this can be very expensive. Many manufacturers forego the patent process altogether and instead use those resources to market their product(s).

A "provisional patent" also known as a "provisional patent application" or "PPA" is NOT a patent. It is just a tool that can be used, often effectively, to lock in a filing date for an actual utility patent. For example, if an inventor has an invention but doesn't want to spend the money now to file a proper utility patent application but wants to secure today's date as the day she files the application so nobody beats her to it, she can file a "provisional." As long as an actual utility patent application is filed within the next 12 months, then the date of that patent is backdated to the date the PPA was originally filed. (Note: This does not apply to Design Patents.)

The use of a PPA also has other advantages. First, you may use "Patent Pending" on the product information. Second, the details of the "provisional" patent are not public. If someone wishes to design around your claim, he cannot read your claim to do so. The patent office doesn't even read the provisional patent application unless you eventually file a non-provisional utility patent application. Plus, now that the invention is "Patent Pending" it can be discussed publicly (with manufacturers, licensors, engineers, even prospective customers, etc.) for a year without risk of losing patentability rights. And the people with whom you share this information have no way to tell what the nature of your patent is. For all they know, your $110 provisional patent application could be a $20,000 pending utility application filing.

The filing fee for a provisional patent application is just $110 (as of the printing of this book) and, while we normally use an attorney to file them so they are part of the filing process from the beginning, you can do this yourself.

The USPTO has information about how to file a provisional patent application (http://www.uspto.gov/patents/resources/types/provapp.jsp).

Other inexpensive resources include www.patentwizard.com (Click on the tinyurl.com link to go directly to the Provisional Patent page: http://tinyurl.com/94dv2n3) and www.legalzoom.com (Click on the tinyurl.com link to go directly to the Provisional Patent page: http://tinyurl.com/96ylll6). Keep in mind, this is best done once you have decided that you are likely to proceed with this product. You have only 12 months to leverage this tool.

The primary benefits of a good patent are for inventors who have the financial wherewithal to defend the product and those who wish to license their products to other companies. The patent is an asset that the manufacturer / licensee will agree to pay for, either up-front or in the form of a sales royalty.

For those people who plan to take a product to market themselves, a patent is often not worth the expense. The same money can instead go toward product development and marketing. However, the decision needs careful consideration.

For inventors who wish to take their product to market themselves as opposed to licensing it, a patent is NOT REQUIRED. Most products on today's shelves are not patented. Surprised? Visit Target or Walmart and look at different products' packaging. How many mention "Patented" or "Patent Pending"?

However, this fact makes market research, consumer feedback, and other methods described in this book even more critical.

Sometimes people will begin manufacturing their product and then license it later to another manufacturer. If this is a personal goal, you should know that, in the United States, you have one year to file a patent after you publicly disclose your product. If you don't file within that year, you will not be able to file this exact product. However, if you've made significant changes to the product, you may be able to file a patent application on the new elements you have "invented" during that time. This is another good discussion to have with a patent attorney.

Trademarks "™"
According to the USPTO.gov, "a trademark is a word, phrase, symbol or design, or a combination of words, phrases, symbols or designs, that identifies and distinguishes the source of the goods of one party from those of others."

Trademarks are very different from patents. In some ways we think trademarks are more valuable, especially if you will be building a brand or have a clever product name. Trademarks work based on whether there is likelihood that consumers will be confused in the marketplace. They are really based on market perception, not the legalese of a claim as with patents.

The other great thing about trademarks is that they can be claimed without spending any money. (First check http://www.uspto.gov to see if your trademark name is being used.) If you are confident that there is no conflict with another trademark, simply start using your brand or product name in commerce and put the ™ mark after it. [Create the raised TM by typing TM between parentheses ( ) and Microsoft Word automatically raises it to have the appearance (e.g., Mom Invented™).]

If you have a specific product name you think is relevant and worthwhile, search trademarks at uspto.gov. Include similar names and products in your search.

Be sure to write down the date and any image (e.g. logo) when you first start using the "TM" with your product in commerce. When you file for federal registration in the future, you will be required to provide this information.

Legally, this asserts ownership of the mark. However, in the event of a conflict, proof of ownership can still be a challenge. Therefore, similar to patents, trademarks can be registered with the United States Patent and Trademark Office. This is much less expensive than a patent and is faster. Once the mark has been approved, you can use the Registered symbol ® in place of the TM using the same process to create the raised "r" (e.g. Mom Invented®).

Go to www.TamaraMonosoff.com/Guides to watch a video tutorial on how to conduct a trademark search to see if your company or product name is available.

Note that trademarks are registered by product category. Therefore, even if someone has registered a similar name to yours in one category, you could still register your item in a different category, assuming it does fit into that category. For example, if I trademarked Lemon Lime Aide drink in the beverage category, another person could trademark Lemon Lime Aide Lip Gloss as that would fall into a different category.

NOW THAT YOU HAVE DONE SOME LEGAL SLEUTHING, BASED ON WHAT YOU HAVE FOUND, RANK YOUR PRODUCT ON ITS "POTENTIAL FOR OBTAINING INTELLECTUAL PROPERTY" SCALE.

LOW		HIGH
1	2	3

Now that you have a good foundation of knowledge as to the existing patent claims and trademarks, we will go into the manufacturability of your product in Step 5.

STEP 5: MANUFACTURABILITY: HOW COMPLEX WILL IT BE TO PRODUCE YOUR PRODUCT?

> **The purpose of this section is to help you understand the degree of complexity and estimated costs of producing the product.**

Any product can actually be made for some price. However, the challenge we face in the product business is to find a way to make great products in a way that the wholesale and retail prices are low enough that customers will buy them.

We have seen products that were developed without this kind of up-front research that ended up costing the inventor $100,000 just to produce the injection mold needed to mass-produce the product. To be clear, that was before a single unit was produced!

We want you to know roughly how much things are going to cost BEFORE you decide to bring your product to market so that you can plan ahead and make sure that it still makes sense to move forward.

Because your product is new, getting close to the actual design costs and the manufacturability will nearly always require outside expertise.

In fact, one of the greatest challenges, and hence, risks of a product business is the fact that technical design and production requires technical expertise that most individuals lack.

What is an Injection Mold?

If your product is to be made out of plastic, your initial professional prototype will most likely be hand-tooled by a handyman, machinist, or an engineer. This prototype will help you create a functional product. Tamara's first product, the TP Saver, went through eight hand-tooled renditions before it was perfected and ready to take to the next stage. It was at this point that an injection mold was needed to allow for mass production. A mold is a block of steel with a cavity that is created in the shape of your product. A machine is programmed electronically with the specifications from your CAD (computer aided drawings created by an engineer) drawings to cut the cavity out of the steel. (This is why good design specs are so important!)

Once you have your steel mold, plastic pellets are put into the mold and heated until they melt, turning into hot liquid. This hot liquid then settles into the mold, forming the shape of your product. When it cools and hardens, the product is ejected out of the mold and the process repeats itself until you have completed the number of parts you are manufacturing. A single mold can be designed so that many parts can be produced at the same time. This is sometimes referred to as a "family mold."

(Excerpt from The Mom Inventors Handbook, *p.118)*

Many of the principles and research steps in this book can be applied to ANY business type. When it comes to "products," we are really focusing on those that fall into two categories: hard goods and soft goods.

- "Hard Goods" refers to items made of plastic, wood, metal, rubber, etc.
- "Soft Goods" refers to items composed of fabric that are cut and sewn such as bedding, curtains, towels, and clothing.

While the exact answers to the questions below won't be answered until an expert is hired to design the product, it is important to get some basic knowledge about manufacturability.

Here are some questions to answer:

- Will it be made of plastic, textile, metal?
- Are the raw materials readily available?
- How complex will this item be to produce?
- Will it require a multiple-cavity injection mold?
- Is there technology/electronics involved?
- If textile, how much special handling will it require?
- How many different parts or materials does it have? Can the product design be simplified to bring down the cost of manufacturing? Does it need all of the bells and whistles?
- Are similar products currently on the market? What are they?
- What aspects of your product need to be included in order to beat out the competition?

This is a good time to start developing a network of professional contacts. Do you have a personal friend or family member who is an engineer or machinist? If not, go online and find product development firms you can call.

Beyond your personal contacts, there are many talented experts and firms serving the product design or "industrial design" industry. While we have the benefit of experience in developing products, we also rely on experts to help us understand the manufacturability questions of a new product. In our resources guide that is included with this book, we have listed some directories that can be used to search for firms that may meet your needs.

However, here we wanted to provide some specific insights and introductions to three firms that we know. In addition to providing full service design, as of the publication of this book they each offer very reasonably priced initial consultations, which will help you gain tremendous information around this "manufacturability" question.

Trevor Lambert is the president and founder of Enhance Product Development (enhancepd.com), a design firm offering comprehensive development services for consumer products, from industrial design through engineering and manufacturing. They also have established a "Design for Licensing^{SM}" strategy for inventors seeking to get their invention licensed.

Q: What are your top three tips?

Trevor:

✓ To be successful, inventors must have a broader *vision* on product development, focus on the problem to be solved, and avoid getting in a rut based on the initial concept. It is imperative that they build a team around themselves to get expert advice and direction throughout the product development and commercialization process. This way they can professionally develop their product, gather meaningful research on trends, understand the competitive landscape, consider various price points in a specific market segment, and ultimately develop something that both buyers/distributors will carry and consumers will purchase.

✓ Keep costs down in the early stages by not overcomplicating the design or adding more parts than necessary. Remember, every part bears added per-unit cost in the form of material and assembly and added sunk costs in the form of molds, fixtures, and engineering.

✓ Design and invent for the marketplace. Avoid getting tunnel vision on what the invention should be ... don't get emotionally attached to your "baby." When that happens, it's common to disregard others who are making constructive criticism that would improve product function, lower cost, or make it more marketable or commercially feasible.

Q: Do you offer a special program that helps inventors understand any aspects of this?

A: We offer a free initial consultation (usually limited to 30-45 minutes) and free quote estimates. We also offer customers a one-hour engineering feasibility consult for $99, which can be lengthened as necessary.

Justin Aiello, owner of Aiello Design (www.aiellodesign.com), specializes in many of the early-stage aspects of design and preparing a product in the hard goods category for market.

Q: What are the most important considerations when determining how complex or expensive the initial development will be?

Simply put, the more complex a product, the more expensive it will be to develop and manufacture. Some of the more obvious items that increase price are size (small plastic parts are much less expensive to prototype and produce than large plastic parts), number of parts (more parts equal more cost), and number of different materials. (A product with all parts made out of the same material is less costly than one with multiple materials such as plastic, metal, and rubber all in one assembly.) More complex products may require power (battery or wall outlet), custom electronics/circuit boards, heating/cooling, motors, pumps, wireless communication, etc. Each of these items adds time and cost.

Q: What are the most important considerations when determining how expensive per-unit production costs will be?

Basically, it's the same considerations as above; however, other factors also impact unit production costs. Two of the biggest factors are volume and labor. Volume refers to the number of units being manufactured at once—the higher the volume the lower the unit price. So, for example, a simple, five-part plastic assembly may cost $10 each in a volume of 5,000 units, while the same product may only cost $5 each in large volumes of 50,000+ units. Typically my clients start out with smaller volumes and therefore have to settle for smaller profits until the volumes start to grow.

Labor refers to the amount of human time required to manufacture and produce a product. This is most relevant in time spent on fabrication of molds and time spent on physically putting the assembly together. Typically, products that require lots of labor can see significant savings overseas when compared to US-based quotes, but not all products make sense for overseas manufacturing.

Q: In the early stages of developing an invention idea, what tips or suggestions can you offer to help someone gauge the likely design and per-unit production costs?

One of the first and most critical steps is determining the estimated retail cost of the proposed invention. This will allow an inventor to determine if the cost of the invention is justified by the end user. For example, if an inventor came up with a great new kind of teeth-cleaning system but then determined it would cost $1,000 per unit retail, they are going to have a very difficult time selling to the average consumer.

One of the easiest ways to estimate the retail cost of a manufactured unit is to find an existing manufactured product of similar complexity and use that price as comparison. For example, if your product needs to heat and dispense water, look at the retail cost of coffee makers. Try to find existing products that have similarities in size, complexity, functionality, etc.

Q: How do engineers get cost quotes?

The only real/accurate way to obtain production costs is to have it quoted by contract manufacturers. If you have an assembly made of plastic parts, you need to get a quote from a contract injection molding company. If your invention has electronics, you need to provide engineering documentation to get the price of a manufactured circuit board.

Manufacturers cannot quote products from verbal descriptions or concept drawings. Instead, they need to be provided with CAD files and/or engineering documentation.

This documentation provides all of the details of each part and includes geometry, size, volume, material, dimensions, color, finish, hardware, and assembly procedure to name a few.

Q: Can this be done in a way that our readers can achieve this?

Without the proper engineering documentation, obtaining real production costs is not possible. It would be like asking a home builder to give you a price to build a custom home without having plans. The best option is to look to similar products out in the market for cost comparison.

Q: What are the biggest mistakes people make when designing and planning their new product?

One of the most important principles in concepting a new invention is "Keep It Simple." I see a lot of inventors adding unnecessary technology ("everything but the kitchen sink" syndrome) because they think it makes the product better. For example, I worked with an inventor that wanted to add solar panels to a battery-powered device so that the device would never need to be charged. In reality, solar technology is very costly and very large and would have made the product too expensive and too big for any chance of success in the market. Spend time brainstorming ways to simplify the invention, not adding bells and whistles.

Q: What else would you like to add?

I always tell inventors that it's not an easy road to create a successful invention. I can help them protect, develop, and manufacture the product, but going out into the world and selling or licensing the product will be their responsibility. I think their chances of success are increased if any or all of the following are true:

- It's a simple, lower cost product.
- Inventor has sales and marketing experience.
- The invention is in an industry in which the inventor is very familiar. (For example, the inventor worked as a baker his or her whole life and came up with a baking-related invention.)
- The inventor has contacts with people who can help get their product on the retail shelf. (For example, the inventor's brother-in-law is a buyer for Home Depot and comes up with a DIY product that would be perfect for this retail environment.)
- The inventor has partners to help share the financial risk and increase contacts.
- The inventor can look at this as an enjoyable learning experience without putting themselves at financial risk.

Q: What steps do you take as an engineer to answer these questions?

Once I have a complete understanding of the proposed invention (from the inventor), I provide them with an Invention Development Estimate (design, engineering, and prototyping). This way, my clients know upfront the cost to get a working prototype. Once the prototype is perfected, we create the necessary engineering documentation to send out to contract manufacturers for production quotes. At that point, the client will know the exact cost to move into production.

Q: Do you offer a special program of any kind that helps inventors understand any aspects of this?

Yes. I offer free consultations and Invention Development Estimates to anyone who calls and I'm happy to answer any questions.

Many new products are "soft-goods." **Michael Thomas**, owner of Choices Apparel (www.choicesapparel.com), has extensive knowledge and experience in designing and manufacturing a wide range of soft goods, both domestically and overseas.

Q: What are the most important considerations when determining how complex or expensive the initial development will be?

There is no real exact answer here. This will change based on the industry; however, I tell my customers they should plan to spend about $300-$500 per new style. Oftentimes it will be less, but they should plan for the larger price, not the lowest. No one wants to run out of money halfway through their startup.

Q: What are the most important considerations when determining how expensive per-unit production costs will be?

Your total cost of components including freight inbound, "your time" spent if you had to pay someone to do what you do, labor to make your product, and finally your markup. Once again, pricing should be based on the market price not the price you think it is worth. This is a very hard fact that most who start a business just do not understand. As I have stated, there is no secret to giving product away. The key is and always should be, RETURN ON INVESTMENT!

Q: Are there any simple methods, metrics, or approaches you can recommend to address these issues: design complexity and cost, production complexity and cost, safety/regulatory requirements and hurdles, and anything that can be derived regarding liability and insurance protections?

In the apparel industry, one of the largest issues is that many pattern makers do not know how to sew and the result is that they might make a beautiful pattern that is far too costly to manufacture. In apparel, one should always have liability insurance. Children's apparel has more issues than most. Thus, the new businessperson should do his/her research in advance. Most important!

Q: What are the biggest mistakes people make when designing and planning their new product?

Here are some of the many issues they fail to either do or understand:

Competition pricing: The common belief is to think that they should be LESS EXPENSIVE than the competition without taking into account that a "mature firm" receives better pricing based on many aspects which include volume of production.

The new businessperson should in reality come in at a higher price and offer a "cash discount" to gain distribution so that their price might be the same as, or lower. The key here is, now and forever, you can always bring your price down, but on that same product you cannot go higher.

Q: Do you offer a special program of any kind that helps inventors understand any aspects of this?

Yes. I am happy to offer an initial consultation for a modest charge that can be credited to future services if you elect to use our firm.

If you contact other companies, tell them that you are working on your product plan and will need an engineering firm. Then tell them you are doing research to determine the manufacturability of your product and ask them if they have a consultation program of some kind that would provide you with an estimate as to the likely cost and complexity of your product. If they cannot, ask for suggestions of resources. Getting this information is invaluable at this stage, and you should consider paying a modest amount of money for good information.

If you come across great resources, please e-mail them to: (info@TamaraMonosoff.com) as we would love to be able to share them with others.

RANK THE EASE OF MANUFACTURING

1	2	3
VERY DIFFICULT, MULTIPLE PARTS & MATERIALS	EASILY PRODUCED, ACCESS TO MATERIALS, SMALL NUMBER OF PARTS	

As mentioned by our experts, regulatory and safety issues are related to manufacturability. Therefore, the next step focuses specifically on how to find the safety and regulatory information specific to your product.

STEP 6: WHAT ARE THE SAFETY & REGULATORY ISSUES YOU NEED TO UNDERSTAND?

The purpose of this section is to uncover and understand the requirements and challenges you will face involving safety and regulatory issues.

As you begin evaluating safety issues related to your product, consider approaching it from this point of view:
- ❏ You don't want to harm anyone.
- ❏ You want to produce a quality product.
- ❏ You don't want to incur liability.
- ❏ You do want to do what is possible to prevent injury.

The way to accomplish this is to:
- ❏ Study the Product
  - Is there a federal regulation or test requirement?
  - Is there a voluntary standard?
  - Is there precedent or history?
  - Common sense?
- ❏ Good Design
  - Design with safety in mind.
- ❏ Test
  - Have your product tested by professionals to ensure safety.
- ❏ Insurance
  - Purchase liability insurance.

Federal Regulation
There are several ways to learn of the existing federal regulations. The Consumer Product Safety Commission is an important resource for companies developing new products. The CPSC is charged with "protecting the public from unreasonable risks of injury or death from thousands of types of consumer products under the agency's jurisdiction." www.cpsc.gov

The first step is to visit the new Consumer Product Safety Commission website. The CPSC site has succeeded in putting data about federal regulations you will need at this stage all in one place.

1. Review the recalls on the home page and get a sense of issues that are occurring with product recalls. (http://www.cpsc.gov/)

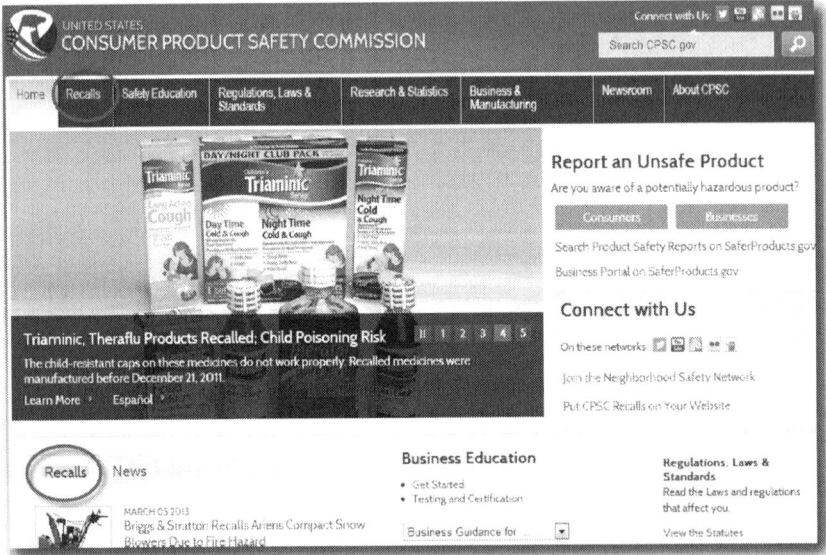

2. On the home page, scroll down to the bottom and review the various safety guides to see if there is one specifically relevant to your product. (http://www.cpsc.gov/en/Safety-Education/Safety-Guides/)

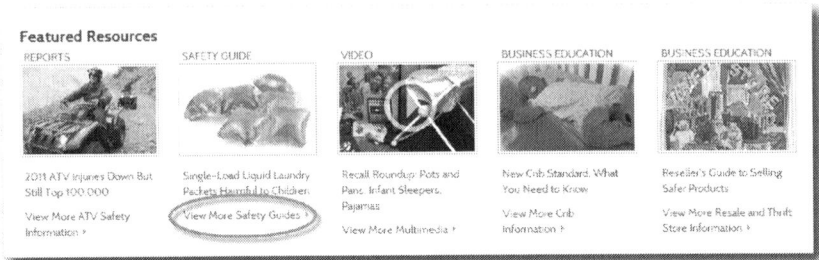

3.   Next you will go to "Business Education" and click "Get
     Started." (http://www.cpsc.gov/Regulations-Laws--
     Standards/CPSIA/The-Consumer-Product-Safety-
     Improvement-Act/#ClassifyYourProduct)

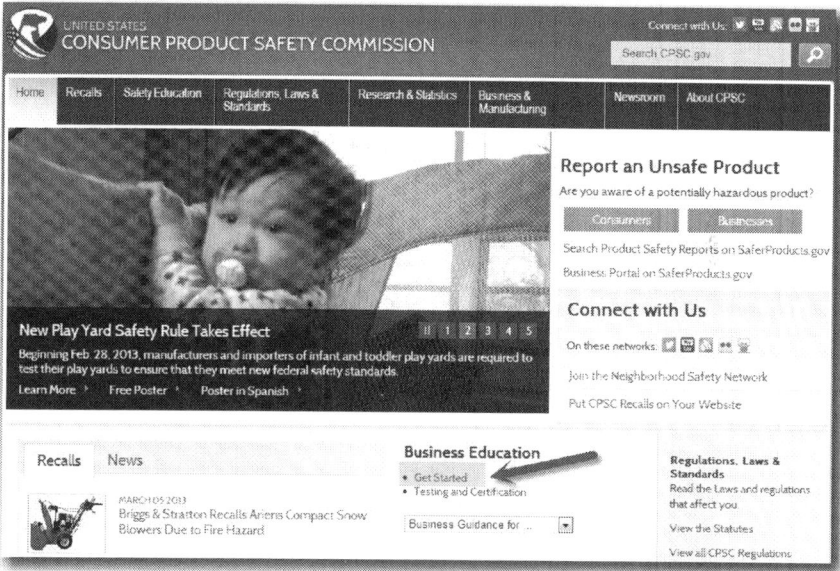

There are two forms of which you should be aware although
this has more to do with the actual stage should you elect to
launch your product. The first is for children's products and is
called the **Written Children's Product Certificate**. The
second is called a **General Certificate of Conformity for
non-children's items.**

It will be important to know whether your item is considered
a children's item. This web page will walk you through the
process of classifying your product and will also provide the
list of key substantive requirements just below the
classification process. (That used to take hours to cobble
together on the old CPSC website!)

**Scroll down farther and see the same information for
non-children's products.**

4. Now, either scroll to the bottom of the page and click "CPSC Lab Search" or go back to the home page and under "Business Education" click "Testing and Certification." After you land there, you will click "list of accredited test labs." (http://www.cpsc.gov/cgi-bin/labsearch/Default.aspx)

- 16 CFR Part 1203, Bicycle Helmets (effective date 02/10/2010)
- 16 CFR Part 1215, Infant Bath Seats (effective date 12/07/2010)
- 16 CFR Part 1216, Infant Walkers (effective date 12/21/2010)
- 16 CFR Part 1217, Safety Standard for Toddler Beds (effective date 10/20/2011)
- 16 CFR Part 1219, Safety Standard for Full-Size Cribs (effective date 06/28/2011)
- 16 CFR Part 1220, Safety Standard for Non-Full-Size Cribs (effective date 06/28/2011)
- 16 CFR part 1221, Safety Standard for Play Yards (effective date 06/10/2013)
- 16 CFR part 1224, Safety Standard for Portable Bedrails (effective date 06/10/2013)

- 16 CFR Part 1303, Lead Paint (effective date 12/21/2008)1
- 16 CFR Part 1420, Requirements for All-Terrain Vehicles (Stayed until November 27, 2011, provided that the manufacturer meets certain conditions.)2
- 16 CFR Part 1500.86(a)(5), Clacker Balls (effective date 07/29/2010)
- 16 CFR Part 1500.86(a)(7) and (8), Dive Sticks and Other Similar Articles (effective date 02/10/2010)
- 16 CFR Part 1501, Small Parts Rule (effective date 02/15/2009)
- 16 C.F.R. Part 1505, Electrically Operated Toys or Articles (effective date 07/29/2010)
- 16 CFR Part 1510, Rattles (effective date 02/10/2010)
- 16 CFR Part 1511, Pacifiers (effective date 01/20/2009)

- 16 CFR Part 1512, Bicycles (effective date 08/15/2010)3
- 16 CFR Part 1513, Bunk Beds (effective date 02/10/2010)
- Test Method CPSC-CH-C1001-09.3, Standard Operating Procedure for Determination of Phthalates and/or GB/T 22048-2008, Toys and Children's Products—Determination of Phthalate Plasticizers in Polyvinyl Chloride Plastic (effective date December 31, 2011. See Federal Register notice of August 10, 2011)
- Test Method CPSC-CH-E1001-08 and/or CPSC-CH-E1001-08.1 and/or CPSC-CH-E1001-08.2 and/or CPSC-CH-E1001-08.3, Lead Content in Children's Metal Jewelry or 2005 CPSC Laboratory SOP (effective date 03/23/2009)
- Test Method CPSC-CH-E1001-08 and/or CPSC-CH-E1001-08.1 and/or CPSC-CH-E1001-08.2 and/or CPSC-CH-E1001-08.3, Lead Content in Children's Metal Products (effective date 12/31/2011)
- Test Method CPSC-CH-E1002-08 and/or CPSC-CH-E1002-08.1 and/or CPSC-CH-E1002-08.2 and/or CPSC-CH-E1002-08.3, Lead Content in Children's Non-Metal Products (effective date 12/31/2011)
- 16 CFR Part 1610, Standard for the Flammability of Clothing Textiles (effective date November 17, 2010)
- 16 CFR Part 1611, Standard for the Flammability of Vinyl Plastic Film (effective date October 19, 2010)
- 16 CFR Part 1615, Standard for the Flammability of Children's Sleepwear: Sizes 0 through 6X (FF 3-71) (effective date February 18, 2011)
- 16 CFR Part 1616, Standard for the Flammability of Children's Sleepwear: Sizes 7 through 14 (FF 5-74) (effective date February 18, 2011)
- 16 CFR Part 1630, Standard for the Surface Flammability of Carpets and Rugs (effective date October 19, 2010)
- 16 CFR Part 1631, Standard for the Surface Flammability of Small Carpets and Rugs (effective date October 19, 2010)
- 16 CFR Part 1632, Standard for the Flammability of Mattresses and Mattress Pads (FF 4-72, Amended) (effective date November 17, 2010)
- 16 CFR Part 1633, Standard for the Flammability (Open Flame) of Mattress Sets (effective date November 17, 2010)

ASTM F963 Standard Consumer Safety Specifications for Toy Safety

5. At this point, don't concern yourself with the actual labs listed. If/When you have your product manufactured, you and your factory will then source a test facility. You want to scroll below the list of labs and read the list of items that labs are required to test for. **Note:** "CFR" stands for Code of Federal Regulation. Oftentimes, you will see a reference to "#__CFR__#." This is how the federal government's regulatory code is referenced. For example, "**16 C.F.R. 1501.4**" is a specific regulatory code relating to whether a

product is considered a "small part" or to determine if it should be considered a choking hazard.

As you may have seen by now, ASTM shows up in a number of places. ASTM describes itself on its website as:

"ASTM International, formerly known as the American Society for Testing and Materials (ASTM), is a globally recognized leader in the development and delivery of international voluntary consensus standards. Today, some 12,000 ASTM standards are used around the world to improve product quality, enhance safety, facilitate market access and trade, and build consumer confidence."

At ASTM there are many committees comprised mostly of industry people from different industry categories who come together to create standards for the development of certain types of products. These standards relate to both product quality and safety. Note that there is not a standard for every product or product type. However, if there is a standard that applies, you will want to be aware of it.

1. Visit www.astm.org

Click "Standards" on the left navigation bar. Once there, conduct searches relating to your product or its category.

2. In your first search, use the key words search window. For example, if we type "crib" into the search window, you will see several standards relating to baby cribs.

3. Farther down, you can also browse by "Interest Area." Each one has many standards relating to that area. For instance, "Sports and Recreation" brings up standards ranging from footwear to archery products to baseball bats.

4. You can also search by committee. Find the committee(s) most relevant to your product. If we select F15, the committee on consumer products, you will see standards from baby monitors to candles to bedding.

5. When you find a standard, you will be able to read the summary of the standard. They are also for sale at a fairly modest price.

Next, visit the test lab websites. We have personally used both www.intertek.com and www.bureauveritas.com for testing. When you go to their websites, visit the "Consumer Products" sections. There are many other labs as well. Spend some time on their website and learn what you can about testing that could apply to your product. You will see references to some of the things you read about on both CPSC and ASTM. You will see your knowledge expanding quickly. Not only do their websites offer a wealth of information, they can also provide consultations on what you need to be aware of for your specific item. They can provide answers to all of these questions:

- What Codes of Federal Regulations (CFRs) are applicable to your product?
- Are there any issues specific to your industry to be aware of?

- What are the labeling requirements for your product? Is a "warning label" necessary (e.g., "This product contains small parts and is not meant for children." "For Adult Use Only")?
- Are there packaging standards / requirements?
- How do all of these differ between the United States and other regions? (Europe has a number of different standards.) Make sure you understand this if you hope to sell anywhere outside the United States.

Once your product is developed, you may need some testing to prove that it meets the pertinent requirements of your industry. For example, baby products have many requirements involving content of chemicals such as lead, phthalates, and BPA. In addition, your product may need to pass the small-parts test, impact tests, or for textiles, flammability tests. These labs conduct this kind of testing and certification. An initial discussion with a salesperson may be useful in finding out which tests they would recommend for your particular product and how much it will cost.

At this point, you will have more knowledge about the safety and regulatory issues relating to your product than 99 percent of inventors. However, we don't want to leave any stone unturned, so you are going to do two more searches.

By now you will have identified the industry association(s) most relevant to your product. If not, type (your category + association) into a search engine. Visit their websites and search "product safety," "product regulations," "product standards," "recalls," and "product insurance." Some may have contact names of product safety committee members who will answer e-mail questions as well.

Finally, don't forget Google. Once there, type "your category" + "standards." For example, when you type "juvenile products" + "standards" and "juvenile product standards," numerous references appear having to do with standards that have been developed for certain (not all) juvenile products.

Next, search with the words below and others that you come up with in order to alert you to problems in the area. Knowing information about these issues before you bring a product to market is invaluable.

- o "Product type" + "recall"
- o "Product type" + "label"
- o "Product type" + "flammability"
- o "Product type" + "small parts"
- o "Product type" + "standards"
- o "Product type" + "lead"

Be sure to note in your workbook all the relevant regulatory requirements, standards, and safety issues you identified.

Even the best manufacturers with top designers and retailers who sell quality products recognize the need for insurance to protect against the unfortunate instance where the use of a product results in harm.

Product Liability Insurance
Under product liability insurance there are two main issues to research: requirements and costs.

1. **Requirements**
   - o Study the industry:
     - Speak to retailers, research industry associations, and contact other manufacturers.
     - Go to small retailers or e-tailers and ask what their vendor product liability insurance requirements are.

- Visit industry associations and related trade publications and look for articles and blogs on liability insurance requirements. E-mail their membership director and ask where you can find this information.
- If you see companies with products in the same category as your product, contact them and ask for their product development department. Tell them that you are an entrepreneur looking for advice and ask them about industry requirements.

2. Costs
  - Contact insurance agents to get some cost estimates for product liability insurance for your product (or to hear about their experience with similar items). If you use the same broker who sold you your auto or life insurance, they will more likely be helpful. Or when approaching a new broker, ask her if she can quote you for all three.
  - Speak to manufacturers that make similar items and ask them where they purchased their liability insurance and how much they pay annually.

Some small retailers have minimal insurance requirements of their vendors (that's you), and some independent and online retailers have none. Most large retailers require proof of coverage of over $1 million. Because Wal-Mart is the biggest retailer, if you are in compliance with their requirements, you are likely to meet requirements of most other retailers. Some retailers have a "Vendor" or "Supplier" tab on their website that will list insurance-related information.

The challenge (and cost) of securing product liability insurance varies dramatically due to the nature of the product. Some items (e.g., baby car seats) are virtually uninsurable, especially if produced by a small, single product company. While a policy for baby bedding can run over $10,000 per year, some insurance is easy to get and relatively inexpensive (e.g., $1,000 per year).

There are three places we recommend to look for information regarding insurance for your product:

1. The related industry association is a good place to start. Contact them and ask what resources and information they can provide on obtaining insurance in this category. We visited www.jpma.org, which is the juvenile product manufacturing association website, and typed in "liability insurance." Among the listings on their site is http://www.york-jersey.com/toys.html, which is a national broker.

2. Contact other small vendors in this category and ask them about this issue and who they use. Trade shows are a good place to meet them.

3. Contact your local insurance broker as well and find out what options are available. In some cases, a product can even be covered by a general policy. However, you should confirm this with your insurance broker.

To see the insurance requirements for Wal-Mart visit www.walmartstores.com and click on the "Supplier" tab in the top navigation bar. Scroll down and click on "Standards & Requirements." Once there, click on "Insurance Requirements." You will see that as of March 2013, they have requirement levels for $2 million, $5 million, and $10 million in liability insurance coverage depending on the type of product. In the same place, they also have a matrix that lists product categories to enable a vendor to determine the appropriate level of coverage. Most items fall into the $2 million category. (http://corporate.walmart.com/suppliers/references-resources/insurance-requirements)

NOTE: When you speak to the broker and request an estimate, you can use the Wal-Mart requirements as a basis for their estimation. They will be reticent to quote you as these rates vary. But if you ask them if they have ever issued similar policies before and how much they cost, you may get some helpful information.

RANK HOW SIMPLE OR CHALLENGING IT WILL BE TO OVERCOME ISSUES RELATED TO SAFETY AND REGULATORY AND COMPLIANCE REQUIREMENTS.

1   2   3

SUBSTANTIAL   MODEST
CHALLENGE   CHALLENGE

In the next section, we will take a look at the financial viability of your product.

STEP 7: PROFIT: CAN YOU MAKE MONEY WITH YOUR PRODUCT?

> **The purpose of this section is to find out if this product is financially viable. In other words, if all other factors suggest that there is a viable market and the product is made, will it make financial sense? Keep in mind, even a great product should <u>not</u> be produced if it cannot be done profitably.**

This is a critical and mistake-prone area. It seems to be our nature to assume that other people will place a high value on our ideas, and therefore be willing to pay more than they will ultimately pay. Some inventors assume that by adding "Made in America," people will accept the price. In reality, as evidenced by the success of mass retailers (Wal-Mart, Target, BestBuy, Toys-R-Us, etc.) who carry thousands of products made overseas, seldom will this alone change a buying decision.

For most consumer products, people are price sensitive. Know that your realistic <u>profit margins</u> (how much money you actually get to keep out of every dollar of sales you earn) are based on a realistic retail price BEFORE you invest time and money into development, production, and marketing. There most likely will be ambiguity in this process because, in theory, your product has not been made before.

Manufacturing companies with production and sales experience can typically leverage that prior knowledge to make these kinds of business calculations. <u>Unless you have made products before, you are not likely to have that knowledge. We are going to show you how to leverage the</u>

work of other experts to put you in a stronger position. That way, you can realistically predict production costs, sales prices, and profit margins.

3-Step Process

1. **Determine what the market might pay for your item.**
   a. Find comparable products and note their retail price points. Use Amazon.com, Wal-Mart, specialty retailers, and catalogs. This will enable you to get the highest and lowest market prices.
      i. To determine "comparable," consider items comprised of similar materials, bought by the same customer, and sold through the same venues. For example, if your invention is a new hand-held gardening tool made of steel, research various garden shears on the market.
      ii. Write down the top and bottom retail price range that you find (e.g., $10 to $7).
      iii. Be conservative. In our experience, inventors tend to think consumers will pay a lot more for their product than is realistic because of the newness or inventiveness of the product. This is rarely the case. If your item is a new lunch box and the market for lunch boxes is $5 to $15 dollars, at this stage it is not prudent to assume that you can sell yours for $25 without very good evidence.

2. **Estimate production costs.**
   a. Hiring a professional product development or engineering firm for this is one method.

We have provided resources in Step 5 and in our resources section in the back of this book.

b. Visit global sourcing websites and identify the overseas price of items made of similar materials with comparable complexity: www.alibaba.com and www.globalsources.com.

NOTE: www.mfg.com is a marketplace where you can submit a request for quotes to produce your product. However, unless you already have a well-evolved product, this resource may not work at this stage. It can be useful later, though, when you are prepared to manufacture your item.

In the search windows of the websites below, insert items you know to be similar (e.g., gardening tools, jewelry, bibs, sandwich boxes, etc.). You will be AMAZED at what you will find at www.Alibaba.com and www.globalsources.com. Not only will you most likely find the item you are searching for but also a list of other, often related items produced by the same factory.

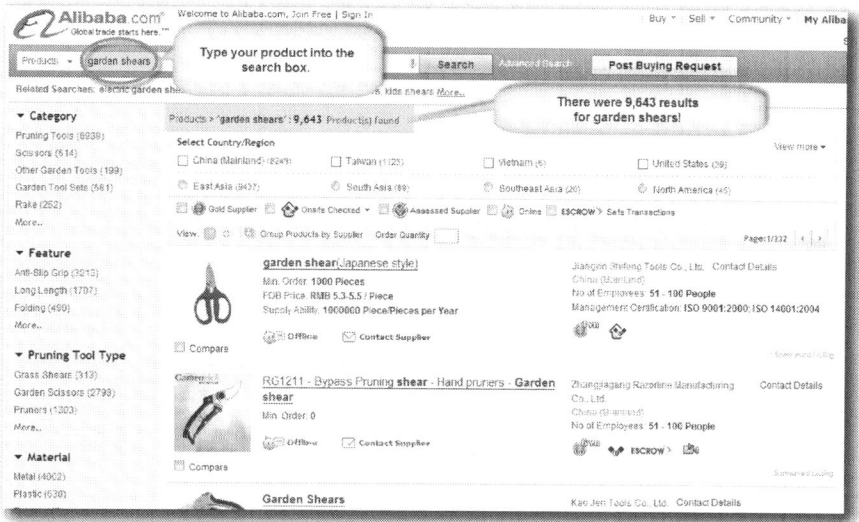

These factories sell these items in bulk. In other words, they sell them to people like you at a wholesale price who will then sell them to retailers or consumers directly. Keep in mind that these factories are already in mass production, so your initial costs with small production runs will likely be higher. Therefore, your own wholesale pricing (the price you offer to retailers) may be higher in the beginning until you work out all the kinks, problems, and challenges that most of us face in our initial manufacturing runs. Also, as you go through this process, make a note of the overseas pricing of items that you think are most comparable to your product.

Some factories may list their products but not the prices. You can request a quote from the factory. We have found them to be quite responsive to inquiries. One thing to consider, even though the pricing they list is "bulk" pricing, be sure to note the volume levels they are referring to. In other words, the pricing they offer may be based on the purchase of 500 units. In this case, you would want to request a quote for higher, custom production runs of say, 5,000 and 10,000 units in order to get a closer estimate of the production cost at future volumes.

Some quotes are listed in RMB, which is the Chinese currency whose primary unit is the Yuan. To convert to US dollars, visit www.gocurrency.com or another currency conversion website to determine the cost. For example, as of this writing, 5.3 RMB = US $.84.

The term "FOB" stands for "Freight on Board." This means the cost per unit when picked up by a freight carrier in China. This does not include the costs of shipping (often called freight forwarding) or other landing costs such as tariffs to get the items back to the United States.

Sometimes inventors are stunned to find their exact product, or one that is even better, on Alibaba.com, already for sale at extremely low prices. If this happens to you, figure out if there is a way to modify your product and improve upon those that are already available. If not, then you may want to let go of this idea and move on to your next one. We've worked with inventors who are grief-stricken at this point and feel they may never have an idea again.

We love the quote from Alexander Graham Bell,

> *"When one door closes another door opens, but we so often look so long and so regretfully upon the closed door, that we do not see the ones which open for us."*

Sometimes when you let go of an idea that has been consuming your energy and time, a space opens for new ideas to percolate in your mind. So don't lose heart.

We have personally met inventors who have spent thousands of dollars on patents, design, manufacturing, packaging, and have hundreds or thousands of units delivered to their garages only to learn when they attempt to sell it that retailers already have access to these items on Alibaba.com or other overseas resources—and at a fraction of the cost. It is important to find this out before you spend a penny manufacturing your product.

3. **Now Add in Tariff and Freight Costs and Get specific information on Tariff costs.**

   A tariff is a tax that the United States government puts on goods imported into the country and goods exported to other countries. It is important to know how much the tariff is before bringing products in from overseas.

Some items don't have tariffs or they have very low tariffs. Others, such as textiles, can be rather high. Visit the United States International Trade Commission website http://www.usitc.gov to figure out what category your item would fall into and look at the import rate (if you were to source overseas). There is a search window in the upper right-hand corner.

For example, sticking with our garden shears product, we went to www.usitc.gov to figure out what the tariff would be.

Step 1: Click on the "Tariff Search Tool" link on the left navigation bar.

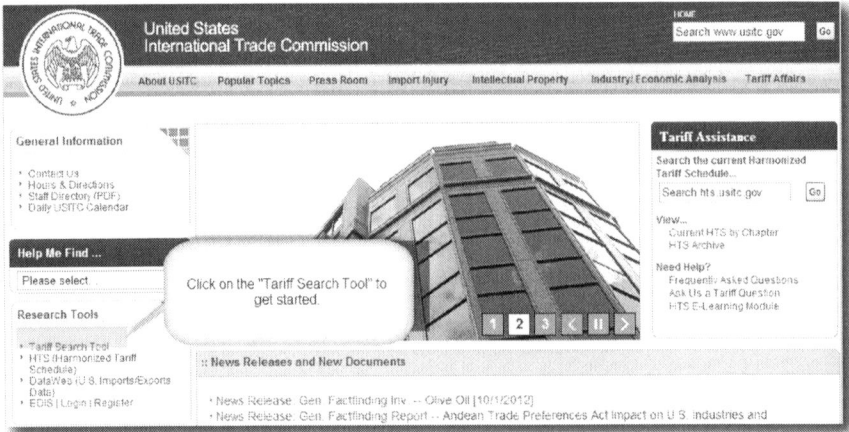

Step 2: Review the table of contents to see if you can determine which tariff will apply to your product. If you can't find it, use the search box in the upper right-hand corner.

Step 3: After you find the tariff code number via the search box, click on the link to figure out the amount of tariffs charged for your item.

← → C 🗋 hts.usitc.gov/hts_search.asp?search_txt=metal%20tools

🌐 Getting Started 📁 Latest Headlines 📁 Imported From Firef...

United States
International Trade Commission

Contents | Results

metal tools

Search Results
412 Results Returned

8201	Handtools of the followingkinds and base parts thereof: spades, shovels, mattocks, hoes, forks and rakes; axes,bill hooks a similar hewing tools; secateurs and pru any kind; scythes, sickles, hayknives, he shears, timber wedges and other tools used in agriculture, horticulture orforestr
8201.10.0000	Spades and shovels, and parts t
8201.30.00	Mattocks, picks, hoes and rakes, ar thereof
8201.30.0010	Mattocks and picks, and parts the
8201.30.0080	Other
8201.40	Axes, billhooks and similar hewing to parts thereof:
8201.40.3000	Machetes, and parts thereof
8201.40.60	Other
8201.40.6010	Axes and adzes, and parts thereof
8201.40.6080	Other
8201.50.0000	Secateurs and similar one-handed pruners and shears(including poultry shears), and parts thereof

It was difficult to find one-handed garden shears. I started with "garden tools" and "garden shears" but didn't find the right tariff until I typed in "metal tools."

Keep on trying different words until you find what you're looking for.

Step 4: Find the amount you will be charged for the tariff. In the case of the garden shears, the tariff is $.01 each (per unit) + 2.8%.

Be sure to include this additional cost into your overall calculations so that you get a more realistic picture of how much this product will cost to produce.

Calculate the Production Cost for your Product.

Remember, in the first part of this step, you looked up retail price ranges. Now, multiply your estimated retail price point (use the lowest price you have found to be realistic) by 20 percent (or simply divide your lowest price by five). For example, $10 (retail price) / 5 = $2 (production cost requirement per unit). If the resulting figure falls within your estimated production cost, your product appears to be financially viable so far.

Now, add in the tariff. If your production cost is $2, add ($.01 + 2.8%) = $2.06 which is the number we found above from the www.usitc.gov website. You may not think 6 cents is a lot, but it adds up when you're doing production runs in the range of 100,000 units. The cost of a production run for 100,000 units (we've received orders of this size from store chains and online catalogs) is $206,000. In that case, 6 cents ended up equaling $6,000 to pay the tariff.

You must also include freight forwarding (shipping from China, for example, to the United States). We typically add another estimated 10 percent to cover overseas and local freight (10% x $2 = $.20 per unit). The price of freight, of course, will vary greatly depending on the size, weight, and nature of your product. So using a $2 per-unit production cost, we would add $2 + $.06 (tariff) + $.20 (freight) = $2.26 per unit so far.

After your product has "landed" at the warehouse in the United States, domestic freight and distribution costs become sales costs and are not calculated as part of your gross margin. Generally speaking, if your production costs are below 20 percent of the retail price, you will earn enough gross profit to cover your warehousing costs.

If you feel you can get a lower production cost, it may be worth getting professional estimates from a product development firm.

What is the estimated retail price range for your product?

_____

_____

_____

_____

What is your estimated per-unit production cost range?

_____

_____

_____

_____

Landed Cost Estimate

Cost Type	Costs
Production cost per unit	
Tariff	
Freight forwarding	
Other	
TOTAL:	

NOTE: Keep in mind that you may start small and ship from your house, but soon you will find this to be inefficient and time-consuming, and the demand will be nearly impossible to keep up with. Therefore, at some point with a successful product, you will need to have your purchase orders (PO's) sent directly to a third-party fulfillment house and they will handle packing and shipping to your customers (retail stores if you're selling wholesale) or consumers (direct to customer if you're selling retail) that purchase your product.

Wholesale Pricing

Up to this point, we have used a short cut to help you determine what your factory per-unit production cost had to be in relation to the likely retail price. Again, we have said that your production cost plus the freight and tariffs to "land" the product must equal 20 percent or less of the likely retail price (as a rule of thumb). What we have not explained is that the reason this percentage is so important is that most product companies wish to sell their product "wholesale" to retailers. This "20 percent" cost structure enables you to have enough margin (money left over after production costs) for both you and your retailer to be successful selling your product.

At What Retail Price Does Your Product Have to Sell in Order to be Financially Viable for YOU?

Have you struggled with calculating your product's wholesale and retail pricing? Do you know how to calculate your profit margins? If not, don't worry. You can learn how in 12 minutes!

There are three key to ask questions when bringing a product to market:

How do I set the wholesale price of my product?
How do I price my item for a retailer?
How do I price my item if I add a distributor?

These questions may be the most important questions you can ask because the last thing you want is for everyone else to make money from your product except for you—a problem we have witnessed far too often. That is a surefire way to go out of business.

To help you, we've created a simple audio teaching tool. It's a margin calculator that we designed to help you get the answers to the questions above. Don't panic when you hear the words "margin calculator." No math or accounting knowledge is required.

This audio is intended for non-business people. After 12 minutes you will have a better understanding of how product pricing works and how to choose the best price point for your item. **Go to www.TamaraMonosoff.com/Guides to watch this useful tutorial or click on the link: http://www.screencast-o-matic.com/watch/cXhIqBbHe**. If you find this tutorial helpful and you want to create your own spreadsheet to do the calculations, you are welcome to do so. The actual Margin Calculator shown in the tutorial is available at www.TamaraMonosoff.com for $19.95. However, it is our gift to you with the purchase of this book.

In summary, when we evaluate the viability of an item, we like to see the production cost below one-fifth (and even better at one-sixth) the retail price we believe price-sensitive customers will pay. Another way to look at it is that you should be able to multiply your product production cost by 5 (or 6) and that resulting number should equal or be below your anticipated retail price. The reason for this number is that when you sell wholesale (to other retailers), they will usually require at least a 50 percent ("keystone") margin, also known as a 100 percent markup. In other words, if the suggested retail price is $20, the retailer will ask you for a wholesale (sometimes called "keystone" price) of $10 (often with other costs they charge too!). Therefore, you need the 5x (to 6x) margin to make a meaningful profit.

Note: Once you have done the math, validation of your assumed retail price by real consumers is important.

Below is an example of how this might look for a product that retails for $20.

You Sell Wholesale to Retailer	You Sell Wholesale to Distributor Who Then Sells to Retailer
$20 Retail price paid by customer	$20 Retail price paid by customer
$10 Wholesale price paid to you by retailer per unit	$10 Paid to distributor by retailer per unit
_____	$7 Distributor pays you $7
$4 The production cost that you pay your factory per unit	$4 The production cost that you pay your factory per unit
You earn $6 Gross Profit Margin (60% Gross Margin)	You earn $3 Gross Profit Margin (43% Gross Margin)

NOTE: When a distributor is involved, a retailer may not expect a full keystone markup. In other words, a keystone markup is any item selling at twice the price for what it was bought for (i.e., a retailer buys something from you for $10 and sells it to their customers for $20). However, when a distributor is involved, the retailer may tolerate a smaller margin because the distributor needs to earn money too. To calculate Gross Profit Margin divide the profit ($7 - $4 = $3 gross profit) by your sale price ($7) or ($3 / $7 = .428). To convert a decimal into a percentage multiply by 100. Therefore .428 x 100 = 42.8% rounded to 43%.

How Do You Find Out How Much Consumers Will Pay?

After looking at comparable items online and in stores, ask people (other than your friends and family), "Would you pay $___ for this item?" One cautionary note: Most people say "yes." They don't want to hurt your feelings or offend you (especially if you consider the product "your baby" and you tell them how long and hard you've been working on it). Ask them to be brutally honest and tell them it will not hurt your feelings in any way. If your retail price assumption is too high, ask them what they would honestly pay for it. Trust us; it's better to learn this now. If it becomes apparent that you cannot produce your product at a cost that provides sufficient profit margin, you may need to change the product, change the approach, or abandon it.

TIP: If a change in your approach is necessary because of pricing, one angle to look at might be to focus on direct sales. This means you would sell directly to consumers at consumer trade shows and online. While you then earn the retailer's portion of the margin, it is very hard to get a high volume of sales this way. So this approach is most feasible for high-priced items. Alternatively, sales through large distributors can improve volume but it severely cuts your gross margin.

RANK THE POTENTIAL PROFITABILITY OF YOUR ITEM.

1	2	3
LOW		HIGH
ADEQUATE MARGINS ARE DIFFICULT TO ACHIEVE		ADEQUATE MARGINS ARE HIGHLY ACHIEVABLE

In the next section, you will look at competition.

STEP 8: COMPETITION:
WHO IS YOUR COMPETITION?

> **The purpose of this section is to help you think through the competitive challenges you will face and your approaches to overcome them.**

This step is very short because beyond examining the current market and the major companies who sell similar items to yours, there is not too much that can be done regarding the competition. However, whether you plan to manufacture the product yourself and sell wholesale to retailers or direct to consumers or license the item to another manufacturer, this is a very important step.

Competition is a reality in business. And the truth is that the more successful you are, the more likely you are to face competition. In other words, it is nearly unavoidable. However, because product development is expensive, it would be preferable to know of existing competing products and major competition before deciding whether to make an investment. Even if all the other pieces of your analysis make sense, if a major competitor has a lock on the market, you may find yourself severely handicapped.

The good news is that, because product development is expensive, it is not unusual for competitors to wait to see if you are successful before they decide to develop and launch a competing item. This gives you some time to capture the market. And if you are able to do a good job, you could potentially box out the competition and create a brand consumers prefer. Or this is the point when a lot of small companies sell or license their product rights to the competition.

In this scenario, where you find that you have an opportunity to launch without competition, rest assured that as soon as you start to secure large retail accounts or generate sales traction directly with consumers, major players will see an opportunity and go after this business as well.

For this reason, it is useful to know which companies make products that are in the same category and would therefore represent likely threats. For example, when I launched my TP Saver, it was the only thing like it on the market. However, there are two or three major manufacturers who focus on items for baby safety. We watched them very closely after we launched. And, sure enough, after about 24 months, one of these companies launched an item that was directly competitive (with language on the packaging that was uncannily similar to ours). Keep in mind that we had a strong utility patent and a trademark, yet the competition was able to design around ours and create a similar product with a similar name. Fortunately, we had enough time to generate our best sales during those first two years and launch additional products as well.

It is time to put on your detective hat. The answers to these questions will be found through research.

- How are people currently solving the problem that your product solves?

- What gave you this idea? In other words, what problem does your product solve?

- What products or processes will your product replace/eliminate?

- What advantages does your product have over others already on the market?

- What directly competing products are on the market?

- Which companies are making and distributing them?

- How many companies are you competing with?

- How large are they? What is their advantage?

- How well placed are they with your ideal distribution channels?

- Which channels have they not secured?
  - Can you find out why they have not yet penetrated those channels?

- How well liked are the similar products in the industry? With customers? With retailers?

- How will you differentiate your product from others that are already on the market?

Visit websites of the companies you know that make items that would be directly related.

Go online to both mass websites such as Amazon.com, Walmart.com, and QVC.com, as well as retail sites that focus on your target audience. For example, if your item is a kitchen item, visit housewares e-tailers and catalogs.

At each website, search using words that relate to your item to see what items show up. For instance, if your item was a child's shoe storage item, search using the words, "children + shoe + storage." As you search online, use different words and variations of words (grab a thesaurus or synonym finder to help you).

Visit retailers in person and note how much shelf space is given to items similar to yours and the depth of their presence. For the "shoe storage" example, we would visit the Container Store and speak to the associates to see if they have this item, and if not, if they ever have customers ask for this type of item. You should also ask what manufacturers would most likely produce something similar.

Also be sure to do these searches on the overseas sourcing websites as well, such as www.Alibaba.com and www.Globalsources.com. If you find something comparable on these sites, you may have found evidence of major competition. On the other hand, it may be that they do not yet sell in the United States and you have just found a fast path to manufacturing.

If possible, walk the floor of industry trade shows and scope these items out.

Before making the decision to invest in this process, understanding the current competing products as well as gauging the nature of the likely competitors who could also be future licensees is critical. Once you enter the market, you will be swimming with sharks. Learn what you can about them before you jump in the ocean!

RANK THE OPPORTUNITY AS IT RELATES TO THE LIKELY LEVEL OF COMPETITION.		
1	2	3
FIERCELY COMPETITIVE	LOW COMPETITION GOOD OPENING IN MARKET	

Some information from this section will aid you in the next step as you likely identified some distribution channels you could use.

STEP 9: DISTRIBUTION: HOW AND WHERE WILL YOUR PRODUCT(S) BE SOLD?

In this section you will learn the most likely places your product will be sold as well as identify potential challenges.

Distribution is often the last serious consideration of enthusiastic entrepreneurs. Many entrepreneurs focus on how to create the item instead of carefully considering how to "sell" the item from the very beginning. This is because they are understandably operating on the myth that "the world will beat a path to their door" because of the ingenuity of their invention. This doesn't happen! In reality, you will need to beat down doors yourself hoping buyers will give your product a shot. Distribution is the hardest and most critical part of this process when it comes to actual financial success—even when everything else we have covered thus far works.

Here are some key questions that need to be asked EARLY in the evaluation process:

1. Is your product a specialty item or a mass item? With the growth and breadth of the mass retailers and the consolidation and demise of small specialty retailers, this question is complicated. Today "specialty" often equates to "online," "catalog," or "boutique" retailer.

2. Will you sell through mass retailers (Wal-Mart, Target, Costco, Bed, Bath & Beyond …) or other specific channels? Which ones?

3. Does your product require special sales expertise (e.g., health care, technical knowledge)?

4. Are there niche enthusiasts who will sell the product?

5. How challenging will it be to access these channels? For example, it is very difficult to penetrate large retailers, while niche industry retailers and e-tailers may be excited to sell it if it specifically serves their customers.

If you have personal experience in your product's industry already, you have an advantage in understanding how distribution works. In that case, leverage this knowledge. If you do not, the following suggestions are meant to help you gain that understanding by engaging with others, across a broad spectrum, who possess that knowledge.

In order to get insight into these questions, start with these assumptions:

Retail buyers, especially mass retail buyers, are not rewarded for taking risks on new, unproven products. They are expected to grow their categories while minimizing risk. Therefore, new standalone inventions face tremendous difficulty penetrating mass retail. To begin to answer the critical questions about distribution, follow these steps:

1. Visit mass and specialty retailers in your category to see how many small company items are on display in the section your item would logically hang on store racks.

2. When you see items you think of as similar to yours, do online searches and note all the places they are listed as being sold. Many vendors list the stores where their products are being sold on their websites. Print out their lists and research these retailers.

3. This step may not work until you have a prototype. But if you do, ask store managers and owners, especially of local independent stores, if they could envision carrying your item. Next is the most critical question. If they say "yes," ask if they will be one of your first customers. This is key because it will force them to give you honest feedback. If they say "No," ask, "Why not?" It's important here to view this as a gift and not a rejection. This is an opportunity for you to get invaluable feedback that will help you create a better product. If you think their suggested changes make sense, ask them if you can come back and show them the new version for consideration when the product and/or packaging have been modified. This will help keep the door open.

NOTE: Some inventors are nervous about approaching store personnel with their products because they worry that their idea may be stolen. Most people you survey in this way have no incentive to sign a nondisclosure agreement. So either get over the idea that everyone is out to steal your idea, file a provisional patent, or just ask them to keep the information you share with them confidential.

4. Attend trade shows or visit show websites and speak to other vendors, buyers, and sales reps. Find out about these at www.tsnn.com and www.eventsinamerica.com.

5. Using search engines, find alternative distribution channels and look at what they sell, and how.

6. Search on Amazon.com, eBay.com, Etsy.com, and Buy.com.

7. Review catalogs (online and printed) focused on your category. (Many are listed at: www.catalogs.com or www.catalogmonster.com.) Here's an example of one catalog we have sold thousands of units to and it carries hundreds of items across categories: www.ltdcommodities.com.

8. Check out hobby sites related to your market (e.g., gardening, pet, cooking, childcare, knitting, or home design).

9. Are there professionals or professional groups who would sell your item? (I have one client who sells accessories for casts. Many orthopedic physicians, and now hospitals, sell her products to their patients.)

10. Are there opportunities to sell through direct sales organizations? *(NOTE: "Direct selling is a dynamic, vibrant, rapidly expanding channel of distribution for the marketing of products and services directly to consumers." According to the World Federation of Direct Selling Associations.)* Examples of these include companies such as; www.Silpada.com, www.Nuskin.com, www.Initials-Inc.com, www.StellaandDot.com, and www.Discoverytoys.com.

11. Promotional Products: Companies spend millions of dollars on promotional items with their logo printed on them. Is your product well suited for this? Note that

these companies are not likely to be interested in products that do not have a patent. Here are some examples of promotional product companies: www.Norwood.com, www.Branders.com, and www.halo.com.

Often there are multiple answers to these questions. First, understand that most new products must start with direct online sales, friend to friend, and direct to customers via your own website listing and platforms like eBay.com, Etsy.com, and Amazon.com. Then sales can move to smaller independent retailers and e-tailers and ideally move to larger distribution options such as mass retailers. At this point, you are trying to determine if and how your product will be distributed. The more data you gather now, the better your decision making will be. In other words, if you choose to proceed, it will help you build a rock-solid business plan.

In the next and final step, you will tie everything that you've learned together: the market data, costs, and pricing. You will see if a strong business case can be made. In other words, is this product worth producing? Can you make money with your product?

STEP 10: BUSINESS ASSESSMENT: WHAT IS THE LIKELY RETAIL PRICE & PROFIT OF MY PRODUCT?

> **The purpose of this section is to help you think through the math and to understand in dollars, cents, and units what must be accomplished to achieve your goal.**

These questions will help you pull the data from these sections together and think through the financial business model necessary to achieve your goals. The table at the end of the section will help organize this information.

- How much money can you earn per unit? (AFTER the production costs have been subtracted. This is called your "Gross Profit Margin."

Keep in mind that when building a business, there are many other costs beyond production. These include marketing, rent, legal, bookkeeping, insurance, salaries, and many others. These are paid out of the "gross profit" you earned above.

The money that is left over after paying these nonproduction costs is called your "Net Profit." While not ideal, many new product entrepreneurs do not pay themselves a "salary" until they know if there will be a net profit.

Tamara co-authored a book called *The One Page Business Plan for Women in Business* with Jim Horan. At the back of the book, we included a CD with business tools you can use immediately. Included is easy-to-use, fill-in-the-blank budget software to help you quickly create your business budget even if you have never created a budget before in your life.

Does It All Add Up?

By now, you should have some knowledge about your costs, market size, and your own income goals. In the next few pages you will fill in some blanks to help tie all of these elements together to see clearly how it all adds up.

First, review a few key questions:

- What is your personal income goal?

- How many units do you need to sell to achieve your financial goals?

- Can you afford to produce and distribute this product?
  - How much money do you need?
  - Can you access that capital? How?
  - Where will you have the product made?

- Who are the customers that will buy your product?
  - Where exactly are they?
  - How will you reach them?

- Can you realistically reach that many customers?

  - If your personal income goal is $100,000 per year and you will earn $.25 per-unit gross profit, from which you pay all your expenses and salary, conservatively you will need to sell between 500,000 and 1 million units ($.25 x 500,000 = $125,000) depending on how low you can keep expenses. Some products, especially commodities (any marketable item produced to satisfy wants or needs) sell at that rate. But very few new products achieve that volume. Marketing and other costs tend to be high for new companies. On the other hand, if you earn $10 per-unit gross profit, you could approach your $100,000 income goal by selling just 20,000 units. Hopefully, by now you have some insight as to whether the customers who will pay that amount of money exist and whether you can find, sell, and distribute to them.

Below is a table with an example of an item sold at $30 retail. You can use the outline for your own product to get some idea as to how to achieve your financial goal. When you create your own table, it is easiest to start with the retail price point and work backwards.

The free margin calculator mentioned previously in Step 7 and the example below are useful for conducting gross profit margin calculations at different levels. The difference between this table and the margin calculator is that the table is focused on your personal financial goals, whereas the margin calculator is mainly about figuring gross margins for you and the retailers.

Per Unit	Optimistic	Conservative
Retail Price Estimate (sold to consumer)	$30	$30
Wholesale Price (sold to retailer/distributor)	$15	$13.50
Price Paid by You to Factory (your cost estimate)	$5	$6
Per-unit Gross Profit	$10	$7.50
Unit Sales per Year (your market estimate)	50,000	20,000
Total Gross Profit	$500,000	$150,000

Note: the calculation above was made by simply subtracting each number from the one above it to arrive at the Gross Profit.

The Gross Profit Margin is what you will use to pay for your sales and marketing expenses, administrative costs, salaries, and rent. So when you look at this number, you can determine whether this product will enable you to achieve your financial goals. Unfortunately, there is not a set number you can use to determine how much your expenses will be (e.g., marketing, selling, etc). In our experience, many start-ups keep administrative costs low by managing a lot on their own (administration, bookkeeping, staffing, etc.) For many of us, our warehouses and offices begin in our homes. However, we still have expenses like advertising, marketing materials, and trade shows, which are expensive.

As previously mentioned, there are other ways to add revenue once your business is running. Ideally, you will begin with a product that will meet your goals.

Blank table to plug in your own numbers and preferred assumptions:

Per Unit	Optimistic	Conservative
Retail Price Estimate (sold to consumer)		
Wholesale Price (sold to retailer/distributor)		
Price Paid by You to Factory (your cost estimate)		
Per-unit Gross Profit		
Unit Sales per Year (your market estimate)		
Total Gross Profit		

This would be a good time to watch the 12-minute Video Tutorial on **How to Use our Margin Calculator** to figure out the best price and margins for your product in a wholesale and retail scenario. As mentioned earlier, go to www.TamaraMonosoff.com/Guides or click on this link to watch the video: http://www.screencast-o-matic.com/watch/cXhlqBbHe

Here's what one of Tamara's Power Mentoring Program Mentees recently said about the Margin Calculator:
"O.K., I am IN LOVE with that calculator!!! Awesome tool, thank you! If you haven't played with it yet – I highly recommend it!" — Leslie S.

TIP: Need help defining these financial terms like *Profit Margins, Gross Profit,* etc.? Read our short eBook ***Power Pricing: Demystifying Profit Margins and Mark-ups.*** This has been added as another special BONUS for purchasing this book. It can be found at TamaraMonosoff.com/Guides and on your Bonus Resources CD.

RANK THE CHALLENGE ASSOCIATED WITH ACHIEVING YOUR PERSONAL FINANCIAL GOALS.

1	2	3
IT WILL BE VERY DIFFICULT TO ACHIEVE MY FINANCIAL GOALS WITH THIS PRODUCT.		POTENTIAL TO ACHIEVE MY FINANCIAL GOALS IS VERY GOOD.

By now, you will have developed many pieces to your own puzzle. You may have already arrived at a point of clarity regarding your product. However, sometimes it is helpful to combine all the key elements (steps) to come up with a clear rationale (even if only for yourself) for whether it makes sense to produce your product. The review rating, in the next section, is intended to help you pull the pieces together.

SUMMARY: PRODUCT REVIEW RATING

> **The purpose of this section is to enable you to further quantify everything you have just learned.**

The rating system below can be useful to give your product a candid ranking of its viability. Be honest. Also, have someone else read your analysis to provide their views. There is a place for both optimism and pessimism here. No doubt, inventing and product development is on the front edge of both creativity and boldness. The decision to proceed— especially if the intention is to take the product to market directly—is major. This is a high-risk business that will require many hours—maybe years—and a significant financial investment. And, like any high-risk business, it can be very lucrative.

This assessment is also relevant if you intend to seek a licensing partner (a manufacturer who will take your product to market instead of you and pay you a percentage of net sales). You can use the ranking model on the next page to try to distance yourself from your decision about your product.

At the end of each of the previous 10 Steps you selected a ranking. You can certainly review and modify those as you deem appropriate based on new data you gathered. Now go back to each section and put the ranks after each step in the table below and tally them.

	Category	Rating Potential: 1 (Low / Less advantageous) 2 (Neutral) 3 (High/More advantageous)
1	Personal Assessment	
2	Market	
3	Feedback	
4	Legal	
5	Manufacturability	
6	Safety	
7	Profit	
8	Competition	
9	Distribution	
10	Business Assessment	
	Total out of 30 possible	

* Unless explicitly stated, the views in this guidebook cannot be considered to be professional legal opinions. Our input regarding legal matters cannot be construed to be a qualified legal opinion as to the patentability of a product or any legal issues pertaining to the product beyond our own business opinion.

When we use this scale to evaluate products, we do not consider producing any items that score below 25. Ideally, we look for items to rank 30. However, this is your assessment. Taking a product to market is serious, and other factors and motives will come into play. How you weigh them is your own decision. In fact, that is one of the benefits of being an entrepreneur. Our aim has been to help you step back and gain the best possible base of knowledge possible before making a major, life-changing business decision.

If your item ranked "low," we hope that you won't just brush it off and decide to plow ahead without serious consideration. We have, at times, made this mistake ourselves because we believed in the item so much and we wanted to overlook the facts.

If you have gone through and really dug into each of these sections, you have a much better idea now as to the nature of the risk and opportunity your product represents. You should feel satisfied that you did all you could to make the best decision possible.

FINAL STEP!

We want you to now put yourself in the "Director's Seat" in that hypothetical product company we described at the beginning of this book. Ask yourself the question, "Did this product prove itself to me?" You make the call.

You will likely have one of three answers:

1. Yes, let's GO!
2. Not yet, I need more information.
3. No, the potential reward does not justify the risk. I'm moving on to my next opportunity.

If your decision is to proceed with your idea, you now need to start a new process that includes the creation of a plan. This will outline your steps in product development, sales, and marketing. It will also require you to think through other aspects of actually opening and operating a business such as work space, business structure, business and product names, bookkeeping, etc. On the positive side, given what you have just learned through following the steps of this book, you will begin this next process with a wealth of information that will enable you to progress rapidly.

My first book, the *Mom Inventors Handbook: How to Turn Your Great Idea into the Next Big Thing*, picks up right where this book ends and will teach you step-by-step how to bring your product to market. In addition, my last two books, *The One Page Business Plan for Women in Business* and *Your Million Dollar Dream: Regain Control & Be Your Own Boss* will provide you with the direction you need to launch, build, and market your product business. Visit my website http://www.TamaraMonosoff.com for information on my upcoming tools and programs to support your progress as well.

Now, one very last step: Take a look at your answers to the summary questions in Step 1 of this book. Has your knowledge and opinions changed since that first exercise? How so? We want to know. Please tell us by e-mailing: info@TamaraMonosoff.com.

We truly hope you have found this evaluation process to be helpful. We know it was a lot of hard work as we have done this many times ourselves. You are now equipped to repeat this process with other business opportunities as it can be used in virtually any business endeavor.

Whatever you decide, you should celebrate and acknowledge the hard work you put into making this important decision.

*We applaud **YOU**.*

QUICK GUIDE: HELPFUL RESOURCES MENTIONED IN THE BOOK BY STEPS

Step 1: Self-Assessment: What are your personal goals?

Step 2: Market: What is the realistic, targetable market for your product?
http://www.census.gov
http://www.ask.com
http://www.americanpetproducts.org
http://www.zoominfo.com
http://www.hoovers.com
http://www.yahoo.com/finance

Step 3: Feedback: What do people honestly think about your product?
http://www.surveymonkey.com
http://www.popsurvey.com
http://www.formstack.com
http://www.silverstork.com
http://www.amplifyresearch.com/
http://www.housewares.org
http://www.americanpetproducts.org

Step 4: Legal: What can you learn for free before you spend money on legal advice?
http://www.uspto.gov
http://www.google.com/patents
http://www.patentstorm.com
http://patentgenius.com
http://www.simplepatents.com
http://www.legalzoom.com

Step 5: Manufacturability: What key things do you need to consider?

Step 6: Safety: What safety and regulatory issues do you need to understand?
http://www.cpsc.gov
http://www.astm.org
http://www.walmartstores.com
http://www.jpma.org.
http://www.intertek.com
http://www.bureauveritas.com

Step 7: Profit: Can you make money with your product?
http://www.enhancepd.com
http://www.aiellodesign.com
http://www.core77.com
http://www.thomasnet.com
http://www.alibaba.com
http://www.globalsources.com
http://www.choicesapparel.com
http://www.mfg.com
http://www.usitc.com
http://www.gocurrency.com

Step 8: Competition: Who is your competition?

Step 9: Distribution: How and where will your product be sold?
http://www.tsnn.com
http://www.eventsinamerica.com
http://www.catalogs.com
http://www.catalogmonster.com
http://www.ltdcommodities.com
http://www.silpada.com
http://www.nuskin.ocm
http://www.initials-inc.com
http://www.stellaanddot.com
http://www.discoverytoys.com

http://www.norwood.com
http://www.branders.com
http://www.halo.com
http://www.ebay.com
http://www.etsy.com

Step 10: **Business Assessment: What is the likely retail price & <u>profit</u> of your product?**

For all guides mentioned in ***How Hot is Your Product: Find Out if Your Product Idea Will Make or Cost You Money!*** go to http://www.TamaraMonosoff.com/Guides.

Authors' note:

Thank you for reading **How Hot is Your Product?**

We hope it served you well.

We welcome your questions, comments, and suggestions. If you have discovered a fabulous resource, we would love to know about it. Please send us an e-mail at: info@TamaraMonosoff.com.

If, after reading this book, you've made a decision to produce and sell your product, you will then need to simultaneously work on setting up your business for success. For example, you will need to design, launch, and maintain a website; draft a one-page business plan; get started using social media for business; create marketing materials; attend trade shows; and consider advertising, promotion, and publicity, to name just a few. In order to support you with all of this, the next series of training materials on these topics will launch in the Spring/Summer 2013. If you would like to be the first to hear about them and receive special launch discounts, please make sure to add your name to our list here: http://www.TamaraMonosoff.com

Warmest wishes,

Tamara and Brad

Made in the USA
Lexington, KY
14 February 2014